Max Rostal

BEETHOVEN
The Sonatas
for Piano and Violin

Max Rostal
BEETHOVEN
The Sonatas
for Piano
and Violin

Thoughts on their Interpretation

Preface
by the
Amadeus Quartet

With a
Postscript from the Pianist's Viewpoint
by
Günter Ludwig

And an Appendix by Paul Rolland

Translated by Horace and Anna Rosenberg

TOCCATA
PRESS

First published in English by Toccata Press, 1985
© R. Piper & Co. Verlag, Munich, 1981

Translation by Horace and Anna Rosenberg,
© Toccata Press 1985
Music examples drawn by Elizabeth Valdez
Appendix © Mrs Paul Rolland

British Library Cataloguing in Publication Data
Rostal, Max
  Beethoven: the sonatas for piano and violin.
  I. Beethoven, Ludwig van—Sonatas, violin
  I. Title   II.Beethoven : Die Sonaten für
  Klavier and Violine. English
  787.1'092'4   ML420.B42

ISBN 0 907689 05 1
ISBN 0 907689 06 X Pbk

Set in 11 on 12 point Baskerville by
Alan Sutton Publishing Limited, Gloucester
Printed by Nene Litho,
bound by Woolnough Binders, Wellingborough

Contents

To Marion

in love and gratitude

PREFACE
by the
Amadeus Quartet

It is with a feeling of having come full circle that we recall the occasion when we went to Max Rostal before our Wigmore Hall debut recital in 1948 to play Beethoven's Third Rasumovsky Quartet to him, to obtain his criticism and seek his advice. This he gave most generously and his words of wisdom still ring in our ears. And so we were most touched when our friend asked us to write a Preface to his book.

The three of us who were violin students with Max came to appreciate his tremendous intellectual and analytical gifts. We admired his integrity and thoroughness and benefited hugely from his technical and practical solutions to musical problems. It was particularly when we studied the Beethoven Sonatas for piano and violin with Max that our eyes were opened to the process of interpretation, the ceaseless endeavour to transform the symbols composers write into living and meaningful sound. It showed us the way not only to Beethoven but to all music.

All of us in our student days also performed chamber music with Max in public. That was when we learned from him how to prepare oneself even before the first rehearsal and how to work. No effort was ever too much to probe and search in order to reveal the composer's intention clearly.

After nearly sixty years of concert-giving and teaching, all these qualities shine undiminished, even enhanced, from every page of this book. It is a 'must' for all students and performers. It is a 'must' for all lovers of Beethoven.

Norbert Brainin

Peter Schidlof

Siegmund Nissell

Martin Lovett

TRANSLATORS' PREFACE

The two stools which all translators straddle at their peril are those of clumsy literalness and inexact elegance. We have done our best to render Professor Rostal's pithy and sometimes idiosyncratic German into an English which gives as close to an exact translation as is feasible, but using English idiomatic constructions where this is possible without doing violence to the original meaning.

The German word *Pralltriller* is equivalent to the English 'turn'; Professor Rostal uses *Mordent*, so we have used 'mordent' also for this ornament. The terminology of ornaments and grace-notes generally leaves something to be desired, as all have agreed from Grove onward; Professor Rostal suggested some of the translations that he would like to see, and we were happy to use them. They include:

> *Vorschlag* = *appoggiatura* or *acciaccatura*
> *Nachschlag* = grace-note
> *Nachtaktig* = after-beat.

Other terms, in English and Italian, are those in common use. One remains untranslated; but which lover of the arts need puzzle over the Viennese *Gemütlichkeit* (which is almost untranslatable anyhow, although it signifies a sort of 'warm geniality')?

Throughout we have used mathematical terminology of note-lengths, as is done in Germany, North America and most other places; British usages (minims, quavers and so on) cause some dismay in North America, while half-notes and eighth-notes can readily be understood in Britain.

Many friends and dictionaries have been of considerable assistance. Martin Anderson has been friend, editor and touchstone, and we are indebted to him for many passages which are more felicitous then they would have been without him. The responsibility for flaws and inaccuracies is of course our own. One of us (H.D.R.) was at one time a *Rostalschüler*, and it was an added delight to be privileged to tackle the Master's brilliant and indispensable work.

ANNA M. ROSENBERG, M.A.
HORACE D. ROSENBERG, M.D.

List of Illustrations

INTRODUCTION

The idea and initial stimulus for this book arose from the need to pass on to a younger generation (and perhaps also to later ones) my lifelong experience as a practising musician and pedagogue, to provide clarification on matters of interpretation and stimulus for thought. I am sure I share this concern with many fortunate enough to have acquired long and rich experience. I hope, moreover, that this book might fill a void, for the many publications on Beethoven's Violin Sonatas either contain one-sided analyses or eulogise their value and beauty, with the exception of a charming and instructive little book by Joseph Szigeti,[1] whose approach to the Sonatas is also based on many years' experience of playing them. Then there is a short section in Book Two of *The Art of Violin Playing* by Carl Flesch[2] which deals especially with the last Sonata. As far as I know, no other performing artist has written on these Sonatas.

Szigeti's little book contains much of value, both musically and technically, but his aim was not to come to systematic terms with every single work, every movement, every phrase, with regard to interpretation and technique both in the violin and in the piano part, as I hope to do.

Flesch, in his brief discussion of the Tenth Sonata, Op. 96,[3] does deal with musical as well as certain technical problems; but, first, his efforts are limited to a single Sonata, and, secondly, he hardly concerns himself with the problems of the piano part and those of ensemble. I, on the other hand, have made it my job to come to grips with the details of interpretation and technique in these Sonatas, deliberately refraining from purely theoretical analyses, and also denying myself excessively romantic enthusiasms. Whether I have succeeded in such objectivity I leave to the judgment of the reader.

---

[1] *The Ten Beethoven Sonatas for Piano and Violin*, ed. Paul Rolland, American String Teachers Association, Urbana, Illinois, 1965.

[2] Two vols., Carl Fischer Inc., New York, 1924 and 1930.

[3] *ibid.*, pp. 185–191.

Personally, I doubt that it is possible completely to eliminate subjective views; but I stand firmly by what I have written, and I hope this book may provide genuine help for many of those who have embarked on the search.

Furthermore, I have deliberately chosen to use language that is simple, and easily understood, and to avoid as far as possible foreign words (with the exception of generally familiar Italian musical expressions).

Unfortunately, many musicologists of the past, such as Paul Bekker,[4] Alexander Wheelock Thayer[5] and others, have disparaged Beethoven's Sonatas for piano and violin. This has influenced musicians, music-lovers, critics and general public alike – which has happened also in the case of Beethoven's Triple Concerto. As in advertising, the constant, persistent repetition of a judgment rarely fails to have its effect.

Works that end softly, like Beethoven's Fourth Violin Sonata in A minor, Op. 23, or Mozart's A major Violin Concerto, K.219, rarely achieve the public success they deserve. The Triple Concerto and some of the ten Violin Sonatas are perhaps of varying importance, but are nevertheless very great masterpieces which, albeit slowly, are enjoying ever wider popular acclaim. Today one occasionally comes across all the Sonatas in concert performances, but, as usual, certain works are preferred by audience and players alike: among the favourites are the Fifth Sonata, Op. 24 (the *Spring* Sonata), No. 7 in C minor, Op. 30, No. 2, and No. 9, Op. 47 (the *Kreutzer* Sonata) – three splendid works. But to choose only three out of a total of ten Sonatas seems most unjust. Consider the (admittedly less successful) Sonatas, Op. 12, No. 2, Op. 30, Nos. 1 and 3, and especially the final one, Op. 96 – all full of important and profound ideas. Simply to dismiss a movement as magnificent as the *Adagio* of the Sonata, Op. 12, No. 3 as 'inferior' is nothing more than the naïve and stupid parroting of the judgment of alleged 'experts'.

Far more constructive and justified is the following statement of Sir George Grove, with which I am in full agreement:

---

[4] *Beethoven*, Schuster & Loeffler, Berlin, 1912; English edition published by J.M. Dent, London, 1927.
[5] *Life of Beethoven*, ed. Elliot Forbes, Princeton University Press, 1964.

One of the most striking characteristics of Beethoven's music is the individual variety of each piece and each movement. In the symphonies every one of the 9 first movements is entirely distinct from the other 8, and the same of the andantes, scherzos and finales. Each is based on a distinct idea, and each leaves a separate image and impression on the mind. And the same may be said of the majority of the smaller works of the concertos and quartets and pianoforte trios – certainly of the sonatas, all but perhaps a very few. The themes and passages have no family likeness, and have not the air of having been taken out of a stock ready made, but are born for the occasion. He thus very rarely repeats himself.[6]

Both Flesch and Szigeti also assess the standing of the Violin Sonatas among musicians and critics. Thus Flesch writes:[7]

Beethoven's sonatas for violin and piano occupy a subordinate rank in the general evaluation of his creation. We will not try to determine to what extent inferior performances have helped spread this opinion. . . .

The musical, yet technically less adequately equipped violinist turns with preference to quartet, trio and sonata playing, taking it for granted that in such cases lesser technical means will suffice him. Unfortunately, however, these three classes of composition contain the most valuable works in whose performance the violin is called upon to collaborate. Hence we have the strange phenomenon that what is most beautiful in our profession, whereby in first instance it really justifies its *musical* right to existence, with rare exceptions does not belong to the domain of our best players. Worst of all in this respect is the status of sonata playing, because the habit common to many violinists of beginning their recitals with a sonata by Beethoven (or César Franck), 'accompanied' by their regular accompanist with the utmost discretion, so that they may 'get their fingers working smoothly', can hardly be regarded as a cultivation of sonata playing.

And Szigeti says:[8]

[6] Originally published in Grove's *Dictionary of Music and Musicians* in 1878–79, and republished in *Beethoven – Schubert – Mendelssohn*, Macmillan, London, 1951, p. 112.

[7] *op. cit.*, Book Two, pp. 185 and 76.

[8] *op. cit.*, p. 3.

If we examine the status of Beethoven's Ten Sonatas for Piano and Violin without preconceived ideas, we come to some rather unexpected conclusions. (By the status of a body of works such as Beethoven's Quartets, or Mozart's Piano Concerti, or Scriabin's Sonatas, or Handel's Concerti Grossi and so on – we mean the degree of wholehearted acceptance of these large segments of a composer's entire oeuvre; we also mean the degree of conviction and devotion that the 'conveyers', the executants of these works have shown toward them.)

When the three Sonatas, Op. 12, appeared in 1799, the critic of the *Leipziger Allgemeine Musikalische Zeitung* censured the composer for 'hankering after bizarre modulations, despising the natural harmonic links'. Although we have come a long way from such narrowmindedness and misrepresentation, one finds as recently as 1924 traces of this quibbling attitude in a highly scholastic theoretical analysis of the Sonatas by a German musicologist.

Flesch and Szigeti, both as practising musicians and as teachers, had considerably deeper insight than many a theoretician. But it by no means follows in all cases that the most successful must also be the best; there are, for example, pop singers who have much more popular acclaim and also earn much more money than many a really great singer. Is this then to be the yardstick? It is essential to free oneself from adopted clichés and to make a serious, unbiassed effort to consider the Beethoven Sonatas objectively; enrichment and deep insight will crown the success of such endeavour.

I must admit that I, too, especially in my younger years, did not always hold these Sonatas in the regard I do today. In my period as a so-called 'child prodigy' I had no interest in sonatas, nor was I encouraged to play them, but even later – for instance, from 1920 to 1924, when I was between 15 and 19 years old – I did not seriously concern myself with the Beethoven Sonatas. I was a good *prima vista* player, and had the youthful light-heartedness, even naïve temerity, to perform the Beethoven Sonatas without knowing them properly. I make this confession not without shame, and I am very happy about the general development of awareness (mine included), because today the intensive study of sonatas belongs to the general repertoire and is just as seriously cultivated as the learning of the great concertos and the virtuoso literature. I don't remember ever having studied a sonata during my student period with Arnold Rosé and Carl Flesch. The position is now quite different, and it is to be hoped that the general evaluation by players and audiences will keep pace with this welcome development.

The reader will perhaps find much in my comments that he has long known, in which case it may serve as corroboration. For many a budding artist it can act as guide; and even if it merely stimulates, I shall feel that my work has been worthwhile. I hope that the study of this book may bring enrichment, pleasure – and productive work!

ACKNOWLEDGEMENTS

I must record my thanks for help in preparing the English edition of this book first to Horace and Anna Rosenberg, whose sterling work and personal commitment in translation went far beyond what one might normally have expected. Libby Valdez was attentive and careful in preparing the music examples. Alan Soper and his staff at the Central Music Library, London, were invaluable in tracing elusive references; my old friend Albi Rosenthal deserves thanks for tracking down a first edition of the F major Sonata. Op. 24; and Professor H.C. Robbins Landon was able instantly to locate an obstinately obscure quotation. Guy Rickards offered eagerly accepted help with the proof-reading. For permission to use the illustrations I am grateful to the following: the Bayerische Staatsbibliothek, Munich, for the back cover picture of Beethoven (engraving by Blasius Höfel after Louis Létronne, 1814) and the pictures of Schuppanzigh, Salieri, Alexander I, Archduke Rudolph and Rode; the Beethoven-Archiv, Bonn, for a photograph of the lithograph of Bridgetower (the owner of the original is unknown); the Hungarian National Museum, Budapest, for the picture of Beethoven's Broadwood piano and the Beethoven-Haus, Bonn, for the photograph of his stringed instruments; the Picture Archive of the Austrian National Library for the engraving of Count von Fries (a lithograph by Jean Keller after a painting by Elisabeth Vigée-Lebrun); and the Music Department of the Staatsbibliothek Preussischer Kulturbesitz for the facsimile of the frontispiece of Op. 30, No. 1 (the other facsimiles are in my possession). The music examples in Professor Ludwig's Postscript are taken from the complete edition of the Beethoven Violin Sonatas prepared by Sieghard Brandenburg and published by G. Henle Verlag, Munich, to whom I must record my gratitude here. And for permission to quote from literary sources I am grateful to: Princeton University Press for Professor Elliot Forbes' edition of Thayer's *Life of Beethoven*; Macmillan Publishers Ltd, London, and St Martin's Press, New York, for the extracts from Beethoven's letters from Emily Anderson's complete edition; Boosey and Hawkes, London and New York, for Bartók's introduction to the score of his Second Violin Concerto; Mr C.F. Flesch for several passages from his father's *The Art of Violin Playing*, published by Carl Fischer Inc, New York; to the American String Teachers' Association for extracts from Joseph Szigeti's *The Ten Beethoven Sonatas for Piano and Violin*; Macmillan Publishers Ltd for the quote from Sir George Grove's *Dictionary of Music and Musicians* (republished in *Beethoven – Schubert – Mendelssohn* in 1951); and to B. Schott's Söhne, Mainz, for the extract from Hugo Riemann's *Musiklexikon*.

The Appendix, which appears here by gracious permission of Mrs Paul Rolland, is the text of a lecture delivered by Professor Paul Rolland at the Minneapolis Convention of the American String Teachers' Association and Music Teachers of North America in February 1958. It was first published in *American String Teacher*, Vol. VIII, No. 3, 1958, and well merits inclusion here.

MAX ROSTAL

General Principles

The Task of the Editor of Music

The 20th century has seen very considerable advances in the principles governing the editing of music. Almost all the editions published before World War II are characterized by basic tenets which we find unacceptable today. Then interpreters, teachers, students and general public expected that a successful artist would note in his scores almost everything he did himself – which, after all, had led to his public acclaim. That is why these editions contain purely subjective annotations with a profusion of dynamic and agogic markings that frequently have nothing to do with the composer's original text. Worst of all, these editorial accretions, with few exceptions, are not identified as such. It is thus hard to distinguish which markings are the composer's and which the editor's.

In older editions of violin sonatas we frequently find considerable differences between the piano and violin parts, owing to the fact that violinist and pianist were, as it were, not on speaking terms. This occasionally happens even now, for the separate demands made by the musicologist on the one hand and the pianist and violinist on the other sometimes lead to absurd results. It can even happen that the representatives of these three professions have not actually met, despite their partnership in editing the same work!

Thanks to an increased sense of responsibility in musicians, musicologists and critics, this attitude has gradually changed, giving rise to a demand for a fairer approach to the work, and for more precise adherence to the composer's markings – although the change took many years to develop. Musicians today (probably more than ever before) undoubtedly want to do justice to the composer's intentions. From this development there has arisen the demand for editions of original texts, of which there are now a vast number. But to avoid any misconception, I should like to explain what I mean by a 'vast number'. Many 'original-text' editions of the same works often contradict each other, since editors today base their work on manuscripts and first editions (as far as they are available) which, however, frequently differ. In many cases the composer supervised the first printing, taking the opportunity to make alterations to the manuscript version. The editor thus has the problem of deciding, in each work and in every single detail, whether to conform to manuscript or first edition; this immediately involves the editor in a kind of interpretation – hence the contradictions in many 'original text' editions.

Oddly enough, the pendulum is now swinging to the other extreme: we are concerned mainly with slavishly following the letter of the 'original' to the last printing error, without always grasping the spirit of the work. Critical analysis of the original text (manuscript or first edition) is, in my opinion, essential; for mistakes, written as well as printed, are unavoidable. Furthermore, the publishers of many original-text editions seem to think that they will be hard to sell without fingerings. In my view, such additions mean that we can no longer consider them original texts.

In short, editions should be based on the information contained in original texts, with corrections which remove obvious mistakes, written as well as printed. They may, indeed, also contain individual suggestions for interpretation; but every editorial addition should be identified clearly and unmistakably (by smaller print or brackets). The user of such an edition can then decide for himself whether to accept or reject the editor's recommendations.

Dynamics

Dynamics in music mean differentiation of volume of tone, graded by a clear demarcation of *ffff* – *fff* – *ff* – *f* – *mf* – *mp* – *p* – *pp* – *ppp* – *pppp*, or as a gradual change through *cresc.* and *dim.* Beyond that there are further shadings such as *sfz*, *rinfz*, *fp*, or *p subito*.[1]

---

[1] The abbreviation *pf*, which sometimes occurs in Brahms, has led to many errors: there is no *piano-forte* in contrast to *forte-piano*. The abbreviation

We find that players often tend to make understandable and often unconscious deviations from the dynamics noted by the composer; herein lies grave danger when, used without control or arising from a sudden emotion, they contrast only too often with the composer's intentions.

I am placing this section early deliberately because dynamics, especially with Beethoven, are of extreme importance and have been most regrettably neglected until the present. In many of his works, such as the Sonatas for piano and violin and the String Quartets, Beethoven took considerable pains to set out exceedingly detailed (occasionally grotesque, even bizarre) dynamic notations, which shows clearly how important they were for him. This point is reinforced by a letter he wrote to Friedrich Sebastian Mayer on 8 April 1806:[2]

> . . . all the *pianissimos* and crescendos, all the decrescendos and all fortes and *fortissimos* have been scratched out of my opera! In any case they are not all observed. All desire to compose anything more ceases completely if I have to hear my work performed *like that*!

No musician would deliberately change the notes, sequences or rhythms of an important composer, but when it comes to dynamics many interpreters are unscrupulous; and since in Beethoven's case the dynamics constitute such an important element of his compositions, their neglect or alteration is tantamount to sacrilege. On recordings (let alone concert performances) one can sometimes hear interpretations by important instrumentalists, past and present, whose dynamics do not agree in any way with the intention of the composer. One example among many is the extremely arbitrary dynamics in the recording by Fritz Kreisler and Sergei Rachmaninov,[3] where *crescendi* are readily replaced by *dimi-*

---

means simply *poco forte*. And through this book I have used the abbreviation *sfz* for *sforzando* lest *sf* be mistaken as *subito forte* and to distinguish *sfz* from *sfp*, which is a *sforzando* followed by a *piano*. (I apologise to purists for 'an *f*' and 'an *sfz*'; but the eye might jar at 'a *f*' or 'a *sfz*'.)

[2] Quoted in Thayer, *op. cit.*, p. 396, and Emily Anderson (ed.), *The Letters of Beethoven*, three vols., Macmillan, London/St Martin's Press, New York, 1961, Vol. 1, p. 149.

[3] *The Complete Rachmaninoff*, Vol. 4, RCA Victrola AVM 3 0295 1.

nuendi, and *piano subito* is timidly avoided, in order to steer
clear of possible shock effect. The *p subito* in particular is a
hallmark of Beethoven's compositions, which is usually
changed into a charming salon style of playing – although I
admit that its realization on a stringed or keyboard instrument is extremely difficult.

Among laymen the concept of technique is synonymous
with speed; but for the informed musician the strictest control
and realization of Beethoven's dynamics is one of the most
taxing challenges, and one which – musical aspects apart –
requires immense technical ability. This difficult but essential
task is hardly perceptible to the majority of the audience, and
artists of a pragmatic turn of mind may therefore tell themselves that it isn't worth the trouble. When one meets this
attitude, one can only despairingly endorse the comment by
Beethoven quoted above!

Nonetheless, Beethoven was occasionally imprecise in his
dynamic markings, and here and there they need supple-
mentation. One often finds parallel passages in the exposition
and the recapitulation marked carelessly or not at all, but
sometimes, too, deliberately different. An *sfz* can have different meanings, such as a sudden, startling, dramatic, demon-
strative sharp attack, or as a gentle, melodious accentuation.
Furthermore, Beethoven often uses the marking *sfz* where
there should be *fp*, or even only *f*. An *sfz* can sometimes arrest
a *cresc.* or *dim.* indicated previously, or it can leave the overall
dynamic of a specific phrase unaffected. The marking *fp*
means something different from *sfz*, a differentiation which
Beethoven himself used only occasionally. Rapid composing
and hurried writing can easily lead to such confusion.

There sometimes occur in Beethoven dynamics which are
marked for purely 'theoretical' purposes, as for instance when
he writes a *cresc.* on a long-held chord for the piano, which of
course cannot be executed and serves only as a directive to
musical conception (as, for example, in the *Kreutzer* Sonata,
Op. 47, **bars 115** and **436**, first movement).

The object must be to create clarity everywhere, although
in many cases, despite striving for objectivity, one cannot
avoid making a personal decision. My message is: show more

respect towards text and dynamics. I know that many of my colleagues consider my attitude pedantic, by which they impugn conscientious and detailed analysis and a rendition which is musically correct and as close to the text as possible. I admit that I prefer this criticism to being called inexact, variable, uncontrolled or sloppy – characteristics which would hardly have contributed towards the production of this book!

Agogics

The concept of the elastic shaping of the tempo in the perform-ance of a piece of music by often barely measurable deviations from the mechanically exact metre.[1]

There was a time when a strict, even metronomically exact, rhythm was essential for the performance of a classical work in the accepted style, a misconception which can occasionally be encountered even today.

Every great composer is a true romantic at heart, and our division into 'classical' and 'romantic' can at most refer to certain historical periods. In Beethoven's case we have no lack of evidence of rather wild *rubato* playing by the classical Beethoven. As Bernhard Bartels reports:

What we hear about [Beethoven] concerning metre, tempo, and rhythm is very interesting. These truly artistic 'liberties' do occur to a great man. Whoever has to fight to get the metre should give up music. All rhythm, every tempo, all music is dictated from within. On the original manuscript of the song *Nord oder Süd*, in the possession of the publishers Artaria, we find in the master's handwriting: '100 according to Mälzel; but this must be held applicable only to the first bars, for feeling also has its tempo and this cannot entirely be expressed in this figure (i.e., 100)'.[2]

After his initial enthusiasm Beethoven spoke disparagingly about the use of the metronome: 'No more metronome!

[1] Hugo Riemann, *Musikalische Dynamik und Agogik*, D. Rahter, Hamburg, 1884.

[2] *Beethoven*, Meister der Musik No. 1, Franz Borgmeyer Verlag, Hildesheim, 1927, p. 345.

Anyone who can feel the music right does not need it, and for any-one who can't, nothing is of any use; he runs away with the whole orchestra anyway!'[3] Although he expressed this opinion, it did not prevent Beethoven putting metronome markings in several of his works where their appropriateness is questioned today.

One of the greatest composers of our century, Béla Bartók, used the metronome with the intention of indicating precise tempi to the interpreter. In his works we find metronome markings changing frequently in quick succession instead of rigid adherence to the same tempo. In a letter to me discus-sing the First and Fourth String Quartets, dated 6 November 1931, Bartók writes:

> In the first movement the metronome indication in fact is quite impossible and inexplicable, and in the third movement also I find many incorrect metronome figures. – And here I should like to point out that the metronome markings in my earlier works are very often imprecise, or are not in keeping with the proper tempo. I can explain this only by saying that in those days I dealt with metronome markings all too hastily, and that perhaps my metronome was not working properly.

In later works Bartók often puts *ca.* in front of his metronome markings, an additional notation which I shall use here in the proposed metronome indications for the Beethoven Sonatas, only to indicate that rigid adherence to the tempi is not intended. Bartók wrote the following as an introduction to the edition of his Second Violin Concerto:[4]

> Timings, noted from an actual performance, are given for sections of movements and, at the end of each movement, for the whole thereof. It is not suggested that the durations should be exactly the same at each performance; both these and the metronomic indications are suggested only as a guide for the executants. It appears to me better to present them as exact timings, rather than attempt to translate them into round figures.

[3] In Felix Anton Schindler, *Beethoven as I Knew Him*, ed. Donald W. MacArdle, Faber & Faber, London/University of North Carolina Press, Chapel Hill, North Carolina, 1966, p. 425–426.

[4] Boosey & Hawkes, London & New York, 1941, p. ii (reduction for violin and piano – the full score was not published until 1946).

Beethoven received this piano in 1818 from the London piano manufacturer Thomas Broadwood. Thereupon he gave his Érard piano to his brother Johann and played only on the Broadwood. It later came into Liszt's possession, remaining at Weimar until his death; a year later, in 1887, it was presented to the National Museum in Budapest, where it remains.

Exact adherence to metronome figures is in any case impossible with many works, nor is it desirable. But the relationship between differing markings is of importance and interest.

Anton Felix Schindler (1798–1864), Beethoven's faithful amanuensis, wrote:

> Whatever I heard performed by Beethoven was, with few exceptions, free of all constraint in the tempo, a *tempo rubato* in the truest sense of the term, as required by content and context but without the slightest suggestion of caricature.[5]

---

[5] *Beethoven as I Knew Him*, p. 412; translation freely adapted. There are many other references to Beethoven's freedom of expression to be found throughout this useful modern edition of Schindler's classic, and his survey of metronome markings in Beethoven can be read on pp. 425–426.

Let us therefore make a clear distinction between a *rubato* and what can be called 'unrhythmical'. Every genuine *rubato* takes place in an organic and natural way, so that even where there are substantial changes of tempo the original note-values remain identifiable. A completely sudden change of tempo, or the lengthening of a single note, leads to distortion, and can be regarded only as unrhythmical playing. A *rubato* is essentially an organic development of *accel.* or *rit.* in phrases of varying length.

There are many concepts which belong under the heading of Agogics, such as rhythm, *rubato*, tempo, *rallentando* or *ritardando*, often called *allargando* or *calando*, and also *accelerando*, *stringendo*, and *fermata*.

Before closing this section, I should like to quote the distinguished teacher, Paul Rolland, who died all too soon, and who, writing in the journal of the American String Teachers' Association,[6] observed

> the distance that separates our (generally) 'polite' streamlined approach to the Beethoven Sonatas from that described by Czerny as the Master's performance requirements: certain 'unwritten' *ritardandi* and *accelerandi*, and other eloquent expressive touches.[7]

So within limits, a *rubato* does not automatically have to be considered incorrect or stylistically inaccurate.

Ornamentation

The field of ornamentation, which usually gives rise to considerable debate, can be treated comparatively briefly as far as Beethoven's Piano and Violin Sonatas are concerned, for there are fewer problems here than in, say, Baroque music. We need consider only *acciaccature*, *appoggiature*, grace-notes and trills.

Beethoven indicates rather inexactly the precise note-values of grace-notes, *acciaccature* and *appoggiature*, in marked contrast to

[6] *American String Teacher*, Vol. VIII, No. 3, A.S.T.A., 1958.
[7] As quoted in Szigeti, *op. cit.*, p. 8. See also Professor Rolland's Appendix on pp. 204–213.

Mozart where the difference between quarter-notes, eighths, sixteenths, thirty-seconds, and sixty-fourths[8] have their exact durations specifically prescribed.

Should we always use additional grace-notes following a trill? Are the grace-notes which Beethoven himself wrote short or long? Although the taste of the individual player is of importance here, one may say that Beethoven, in the so-called first period of his work, followed, more or less, the practice of the Mannheim School. Grace-notes thus seem appropriate, though not specifically or separately notated.

The sitation becomes somewhat more confused in Beethoven's middle period, where he very often – but not always – prescribes grace-notes. In his late works (for example, in the last Sonata, Op. 96) it is my opinion that no grace-notes should be played unless expressly prescribed.

In the discussion of each Sonata I shall give exact details of the ornamentation in every case.

Orthography

'Musical orthography is the sum of the conventions in the notation of music.'[9] Thus it is the teaching of proper 'spelling'.

In many of Beethoven's manuscripts, annotations or dynamic indications are not always placed exactly where they actually belong. Even first editions do not offer a clear picture, principally because violin and piano parts were printed separately, that is, not as complete scores as in the manuscripts. Uncertainties thus arose about the composer's intentions, giving rise to very different interpretations. Here are just a few examples of unclear notation: in the Sonata No. 3 in E flat major, Op. 12, No. 3, **bar 23**, all the editions print the grace-note in the violin part before the beat of the first quarter-note. The *p* also does not come until the note F, that is, the dotted quarter. Does the violin then continue the

---

[8] See Translator's Preface, p. 8.

[9] Hugo Riemann, *Musiklexikon*, Sachteil, B. Schott's Söhne, Mainz, 1967, p. 692 (also in 2 vols., ed. Carl Dahlhaus and Hans Heinrich Eggebrecht, Brockhaus, Wiesbaden/Schott, Mainz, 1979, p. 255).

previous *ff* melodically, up to and including the grace-note A, and does the piano's first beat coincide with the F of the violin after the grace-note? Or should the grace-note be played on the beat? The notation *p* in the piano part is also indicated after the beat. (My recommendations are on p. 59.)

In the second movement of the same Sonata, in **bar 19**, a similar question arises, but here the problem is in the piano part. We find the same also in the Tenth Sonata, Op. 96, in **bar 58** of the second movement.

A further example: in the *Kreutzer* Sonata, Op. 47, unfounded doubts exist about the placing of the *adagio* at the upbeat of the violin in **bar 574** of the first movement. In almost all earlier editions this *adagio* is actually printed on the upbeat of the violin, but in the piano part not until the next **bar 575**. In the new Henle edition[10] the *adagio* in both parts does not come until **bar 575**. I cannot advocate either solution; in the first case it is impossible to let the violin begin the *adagio* alone, leaving the *presto* in the piano. How that can be rhythmically executed, the gods only (perhaps) know! In the second case, the rhythmical problem would be solved but the abrupt change of tempo from the *presto* to the *adagio* is musically questionable. Furthermore, the upbeat of the violin would still be in *presto*, while the piano would play the same thematic passage just four bars later (**bar 578**) in *adagio*. In my opinion there is no doubt that in **bars 572–574** a *ritardando* is missing. This gradual calming down leads into the *adagio* much more logically, and makes it possible to realize the upbeat of the violin in a similar manner to its subsequent presentation in the piano.

In the same Sonata there is considerable doubt about the allocation of the rhythm between the violin and piano parts in **bar 196** of the second movement (see p. 154).

The choice of dynamics in **bar 61** of the second movement of Op. 96 is a very difficult decision. With the exception of the Henle edition, all the earlier published versions printed the *p* on the last eighth-note for both instruments. In Henle the violin has the *p* already on the last eighth-note, but the piano

---

[10] Edited by Sieghard Brandenburg, G. Henle Verlag, Munich, 1975.

not until the last sixteenth. This solution brings acoustically insurmountable difficulties. For me there are only two possibilities: both instruments play *p* either on the last eighth-note or not until the beginning of the next bar, as is indicated in any case in the piano part of the first edition.

I have given here only a few instances of the sort of questions that arise from textual inaccuracies. As we examine each of the Sonatas I shall deal with such questions in detail.

Repeats

The rules of composition in many periods held it customary to put repeat signs automatically for some sections of a piece of music, as, for example, in the exposition of a sonata movement or in variations; even in binary movements in baroque music the second section also gets a repeat sign; and most scherzo and dance-forms naturally involve repeats.

In practice today, in performances of movements in sonata form, not all the repeats are always observed, lending support to the view that they are not obligatory. There are artists and listeners, too, who feel repeats to be unnecessary, even boring, in well-known works. The main function of a repeat – apart from formal reasons – is, after all, to acquaint the listener with the material, mainly the exposition, before we get to the modifications and alterations in the development, the recapitulation and the coda. I am reluctant to repeat second sections in every case simply because it sometimes goes against the grain to return to the dominant when the tonic (and with it the close) has already been reached. In each case my decision depends on certain factors. If, for instance, a composer has written out a *prima* and *seconda volta* at the end of a movement, I would respect such a repeat absolutely. On the other hand, there are cases, even in the Beethoven Sonatas (the Scherzo of the *Spring* Sonata, Op. 24, and the Scherzo of the C minor Sonata, Op. 30, No. 2), where in the first part it is expressly noted *La prima parte senza repetizione*, which means not to repeat as convention would require.

Even in Beethoven's time it is said that prescribed repeats

were not always adhered to in performance. How, other than to ensure their execution, can it be explained that Beethoven, in the second movement (*Tempo di Minuetto*) of the G major Sonata, Op. 30, No. 3, wrote out all the repeats, even where nothing was changed?

Let me conclude then that in my opinion it is not absolutely necessary to follow the composer's direction for repeats in every case. But with every single repeat one must weigh the musical advantages and disadvantages, and here form and personal taste play an essential role. Such decisions must in any case be carefully considered.

Fingerings and Bowings

Fingerings, as well as bowings, are generally a very personal matter, for which reason even rather good editions have fallen into disrepute: only too often the editor publishes what – strictly speaking – is right for himself or valid for only a small minority of string players. Such idiosyncracies as, for instance, the preference for one finger, resulting from a weakness or some other cause, have crept inadvertently into these editions. The same applies to special tendencies in bowing, as with, for example, a preference for the upper half of the bow. What is helpful for some players can present an unnecessary obstacle for others. But I do not want to assert that in *all* cases an editor puts into his editions fingerings and bowings which he personally finds easier because he himself perhaps has to contend with certain handicaps; he may have found out by experience that the solutions which he proposes are most effective, as far as he is concerned.

Furthermore, in the playing of stringed instruments nothing seems to become dated as quickly as fingerings, and even bowings. We must not forget that fingerings for string players are generally and, to a disproportionately higher degree, more closely connected with expression, phrasing, timbre and inter-pretation than, for instance, with the piano where mostly it is only a matter of technical advantage. Every twenty-five to thirty years, on average, a change occurs in musical taste; of

Beethoven's stringed instruments, now in the Beethoven-Haus in Bonn. From left to right: viola by Vincenzo Rugero (1690); cello by Andrea Guarneri (1675); viola from Beethoven's Bonn period; violin by Nicola Amati (1690); violin by Giuseppe Guarneri (1718).

course, this also affects fingerings and bowings which thereby become partly or entirely impracticable. Take, for instance, some of the older editions by Ferdinand David, or even Joseph Joachim: we cannot quite understand how such eminent artists could, even occasionally, arrive at such primitive and (for our generation) ugly fingerings. The avoiding, as much as possible, of the second, fourth, sixth and eighth positions resulted in many (for us) unbearable *portamenti*, employed perforce for technical reasons. Today the constant use of natural harmonics, and even open strings, on *sustained* notes is out of the question; but this practice is explained by the fact that formerly vibrato was not only used rather sparingly but was often looked on as a manifestation of bad taste.

Many editors and violinists are prepared to compromise by using 'simplified' fingerings to provide a higher degree of reliability in performance; this, I think, is rather inartistic. Admittedly the aesthetically and musically 'correct' fingering in many cases is also the more difficult, but for a presentation that is artistically and musically clear it is a price worth paying.

On bowings my viewpoint is that with Beethoven and many other composers the written slurs do not indicate bow changes but are only suggestions for phrasing, which I follow without scruple, although bow changes are often necessary, for one thing, given the acoustics of larger halls and the requisite tone production. In such cases I always leave the original phrasing untouched, but I annotate the divisions by upbow and down-bow marks (∨ and ⊓), which presuppose inaudible bow changes. As we know, Beethoven, like many other composers, was a virtuoso pianist and did not have the same knowledge of the technique of stringed instruments. (Although he began his professional life as a modest orchestral violist, whenever he wrote for the violin he always tried to get the advice of a well-known violinist.) Since Beethoven occasionally put slurs over twelve or more bars, even in *adagio* movements, which is not feasible in bowing, they are mainly to be understood as phrasings.

The bowings one finally selects, according to various criteria, should first and foremost serve the phrasing, or the musical presentation itself; only secondarily should they be dictated by technical comfort and security.

If one is prepared to sacrifice musical, stylistic and artistic values, life and safety on the instrument can be made much simpler. In this respect the greatest achievement of recent times is, for me, the acceptance of the highest, strictest artistic demands and the avoidance, through superior technique, of compromises that mainly serve ease and comfort. It is in truth a matter either of technically solid and reliable fingerings with inadequate musical responsibility, or an interpretation which is genuinely artistic though technically often more complex. That synthesis alone seems the only truly satisfactory, indeed, ideal solution.

Suggestions for Metronome Markings

Sonata No. 1 in D major, Op. 12, No. 1
(i)   *Allegro con brio*   ♩ = ca. 76 – 80
(ii) *Andante con moto*   ♩ = ca. 54 – 58
(iii) *Rondo. Allegro*   ♩ = ca. 104 – 108

Sonata No. 2 in A major, Op. 12, No. 2
(i)   *Allegro vivace*   ♩. = ca. 108 – 112
(ii) *Andante più tosto Allegretto* ♩ = ca. 52 – 60
(iii) *Allegro piacevole*   ♩. = ca. 76 – 84

Sonata No. 3 in E flat major, Op. 12, No. 3
(i)   *Allegro con spirito*   ♩ = ca. 126 – 144
(ii) *Adagio con molta espressione* ♪ = ca. 63 – 72
(iii) *Rondo. Allegro molto*   ♩ = ca. 138 – 144

Sonata No. 4 in A minor, Op. 23
(i)   *Presto*   ♩. = ca. 132 – 176
(ii) *Andante scherzoso più Allegretto* ♩ = ca. 76 – 84
(iii) *Allegro molto*   ♩ = ca. 144 – 160

Sonata No. 5 in F major, Op. 24 (*Spring* Sonata)
(i)   *Allegro*   ♩ = ca. 138 – 152
(ii) *Adagio molto espressivo*   ♪ = ca. 72 – 88
(iii) *Scherzo. Allegro molto*   ♩. = ca. 88 – 96
(iv) *Rondo. Allegro ma non troppo* ♩ = ca. 72 – 84

Sonata No. 6 in A major, Op. 30, No. 1
(i)   *Allegro*   ♩ = ca. 138 – 144
(ii) *Adagio molto espressivo*   ♪ = ca. 50 – 60
(iii) *Allegretto con Variazioni* ♩ = ca. 76 – 84
      Var.VI *Allegro, ma non tanto* ♩. = ca. 84 – 92

Sonata No. 7 in C minor, Op. 30, No. 2
(i)   *Allegro con brio*   ♩ = ca. 138 – 152
(ii) *Adagio cantabile*   ♩ = ca. 50 – 56
(iii) *Scherzo. Allegro*   ♩. = ca. 60 – 69
      Trio   ♩. = ca. 58 – 66

(iv) *Finale. Allegro*   ♩ = ca. 120 – 138
      Presto   ♩ = ca. 152 – 168

Sonata No. 8 in G major, Op. 30, No. 3
(i)   *Allegro assai*   ♩ = ca. 96 – 108
(ii)   *Tempo di Minuetto*   ♩ = ca. 80 – 92
(iii) *Allegro vivace*   ♩ = ca. 66 – 76

Sonata No. 9 in A major, Op. 47 (*Kreutzer* Sonata)
(i)   *Adagio sostenuto*   ♪ = ca. 63 – 76
      Presto   ♩ = ca. 138 – 168
(ii)   *Andante con Variazioni*   ♪ = ca. 88 – 104
      Var. I & II   ♪ = ca. 108 – 126
      Var. III *Minore*   ♪ = ca. 80 – 92
      Var. IV *Maggiore*   ♪ = ca. 80 – 92
(iii) *Presto*   ♪. = ca. 168 – 192

Sonata No. 10 in G major, Op. 96
(i)   *Allegro moderato*   ♩ = ca. 112 – 126
(ii)   *Adagio espressivo*   ♪ = ca. 50 – 63
(iii) *Scherzo. Allegro*   ♩. = ca. 66 – 76
      Trio   ♩. = ca. 60 – 72
(iv) *Poco Allegretto*   ♩ = ca. 88 – 100
      (Var. I)   ♩ = ca. 88 – 100
      (Var. II)   ♩ = ca. 92 – 104
      (Var. III)   ♩ = ca. 88 – 100
      Adagio espressivo   ♪ = ca. 44 – 52
      Allegro   ♩ = ca. 116 – 138
      Poco adagio   ♪ = ca. 88 – 126
      Presto   ♩ = ca. 126 – 144

Sonata No. 1 in D major, Op. 12, No. 1

TRE SONATE

Per il Clavicembalo o Forte-Piano con un Violino

Composte, e Dedicate

al Sig.r ANTONIO SALIERI

primo Maestro di Capella della Corte Imperiale di Vienna &c. &c.

— dal —

Sig.r Luigi van *Beethoven*

Opera 12.

A Vienna presso Artaria e Comp.

Dedicated to Antonio Salieri
Manuscript missing
Composed 1797–98
First edition end of 1798 or beginning of 1799

Introduction

This first of the ten Sonatas for piano and violin is as remarkable as the Op. 1 Piano Trios. Although it is still rather downgraded by many musicologists, it already shows evidence of great mastery. The first two Sonatas of Op. 12 do not yet reach the greatness and depth of later works, it is true, as can be said also of other compositions by Beethoven, such as, for instance, the first Piano Sonatas or the Op. 18 String Quartets. And yet, even in early Beethoven the genius can already be seen, as with early Mozart and Schubert. Happily, this First Sonata, more than the Second, can still be heard not infrequently in the concert hall, and is accepted by the public with pleasure. In addition to the musically unproblematic, fresh and formally perfect first and third movements, we already find in the second movement great mastery in the command of variation form. There are here structural similarities to the *Kreutzer* Sonata, Op. 47: in both the first variation gives the solo part to the piano and the second to the violin, while the others are true duets.

All things considered, this is a charming work!

First Movement: *Allegro con brio*

The very first chord is frequently executed differently by the two instruments. Pianists have entirely done away with the stereotyped *arpeggio* fashionable at the end of the 19th and beginning of the 20th century. Regrettably, this is not true of violinists, who still have the bad habit of spreading almost all the chords, which leads to a dilution of the rhythm. In this case there is neither musical nor technical reason for it. If the violinist cannot sustain the three notes as one chord, my proposal is the following:

1

The dots above and below the quarter-notes in the first four bars for both instruments, and in the violin only in **bars 5–9**, are, of course, to be understood as a shortening of each quarter-note in the piano as well as the violin, and not as a rest before the note. To remedy this unclear, ambiguous notation I had the idea of using differentiated orthography for the two types of execution. It can be found in most of my editions:

The dot inside the slur indicates a tiny rest before the note, for the violinist in the first case by lifting the bow, and in the second case on the string.

The dot outside the slur indicates shortening of this note without a previous rest:

Unfortunately in former times this difference was not clearly demonstrated; this is so even today. We have here again an obvious example of contradictory notation and unsystematic terminology!

The phrasing in **bars 14–16** and **18** in the piano, as well as in the corresponding passage at **bars 151–153** and **155**, is played by almost all pianists as if the last two quarter-notes had the same meaning. They usually sound alike and are not differentiated in either dynamic or duration. For me, the first quarter-note in each case marks the ending of the triplet phrase, while the second is to be taken as an upbeat, as it were. I propose therefore shortening the first quarter-note a little more than the second, perhaps:

2

The *piano subito* (so characteristic in Beethoven) in **bar 12** should be taken very seriously by both partners – a comment which applies to the dynamics of all Beethoven's works.

In the first edition we find the *p*, in the violin part, already at the beginning of **bar 21**, which hardly seems appropriate with a simultaneous *fp* on the piano. I would therefore advise the violinist not to begin the *p* until the third quarter-note of this bar.

The *ff* in **bar 26**, undoubtedly meant as a sudden (that is, unexpected) *subito*, should by no means be introduced by a *crescendo*, unlike **bars 28–33** where the violinist has particularly to note that the piano continues the *crescendo* without rests. At each new entry of the violinist after the interruptions, he has to adjust his dynamics to the level the piano has already reached. This is possible by imagining that the *cresc.* continues even during the rests.

The violinist in **bars 34** and **38** as well as **159** and **163**, just as the pianist in **bars 14**, **16** and **18** and **151**, **153** and **155**, should effect a differentiated phrasing of the last quarter-notes. The last but one is the termination of the previous phrase, and the last quarter-note the upbeat for the next phrase; this is particularly clear in the violin part in **bar 162**:

3

In the piano in **bars 36**, **40** and **161** the same applies. **Bars 51–52** and **176–177** again have the unclear dot notation; here, too, one should not pause before the second tied note but shorten it. And this applies, for the piano, to **bars 55–56** and **180–181**.

The triplet upbeat in the piano in **bars 50** and **175**, and **bars 54** and **179** in the violin, should be a little different from the previous phrase because at these points the respective instruments take the lead. At the end of **bars 57** and **182** in the triplet figure for the violin a tiny introductory *calando* seems to me desirable. The eighth-notes in the violin part in **bars 61** and **186** should not be played too short, despite the dots, thus:

4

I would strictly observe the rather individual dynamics of both instruments in **bars 64–70** and **189–195**, for they are absolutely convincing and obviously intended to be different for the two instruments. Only too often the violinist makes no differentiation between the *p* in **bar 71** and the *pp* in **bar 72** because the initial *p* is taken too quietly, leaving no capacity for further softening; this applies also to **bars 196–197**.

One serious error many violinists commit is the habit of effecting a *ritardando* in **bars 77** and **202**, simply because they are the last for the violin. What we actually have here is a four-bar phrase, which is concluded only by the piano, in **bars 78** and **203**. Accordingly, only the pianist – if anybody – can use a more or less concluding tiny *rit.*

In **bar 86** the violinist should certainly play a grace-note after the trill, as is indicated at this point for the piano, quite apart from the fact that at the corresponding point in **bar 211** the grace-note is indicated by Beethoven himself.

The dots for both instruments in **bars 87–88, 102–103,** and **212–213** indicate a very slight separation of the notes; and thus quite rule out the use of the sustaining pedal on the piano!

In **bars 89–90, 104–105,** and **214–215** the last quarter-note in the violin is always a single note, and so is stressed much less in contrast to the preceding chord. This should induce the pianist to give his second chord too a little less emphasis.

Oddly enough, in the violin in **bar 106** the *acciaccatura* in the first edition is shown as an A, but in almost all other editions as a C. Surely what we have here is a printing error, since the corresponding *acciaccature* in the piano in **bars 108, 112, 116** and **120** always start from the lower octave.

The widespread pianistic habit of sustaining **bars 126–132** with a lot of pedal I consider absolutely incorrect, for, apart from the dots above the concluding quarter-notes (which as we know indicate a shortening of the note value), we are not dealing here simply with spread chords but with a variant of the thematic statement as in **bars 1–4** and **138–141**.

For technical reasons the violin chords in **bars 91–92** and **216–217** are often played much too *forte*; they should start really quietly in order to facilitate an intensification to **bar 93** and **bar 218** respectively, which is no problem if an *arpeggio* is played very quickly at the tip of the bow.

In **bar 205** in almost all early editions there is an incorrect note in the violin part:

5   *(musical notation)*   instead of   *(musical notation)*   6

For the rest, I share Joseph Szigeti's opinion[1] that the tempo of this movement should not be taken too quickly, that is, not *alla breve* but always $\frac{4}{4}$ despite the marking *con brio*.

Second Movement:
Tema con Variazioni. Andante con moto

This movement is unfortunately often played almost like an *adagio*, too slowly. Although I am not of the opinion that all variations have to be held strictly to one and the same tempo, I find the basic character of this movement, with the exception of the third variation, rather graceful and playful. As Justus Hermann Wetzel quite rightly says:

> . . . only those who understand that the character is specifically determined by the motifs and treat it accordingly will be able to conjure up the spirit of this music, which is still derived from the rococo. There is pleasure in the playful manipulation of small and very small motifs, and this must govern the performer as it guided the creativity of the composer.[2]

The first and second variations are entirely in the character of the theme and for this very reason should be played in approximately the same tempo. But with the third and fourth variations it is different: the *Minore* variation has something extraordinarily stormy and dramatic about it, and could certainly be faster than the previous ones; the *Maggiore* variation, however, is of a transfigured character, quietly backward-looking, and it might be taken almost a little slower than the theme.

[1] *op. cit.*, p. 46.
[2] *Beethovens Violinsonaten*, Vol. 1, Max Hesses Verlag, Berlin, 1924, p. 57.

In the theme both pianists and violinists should already take note of the various significances of the dots. Pianists seem to be a little more familiar than violinists with the fact that dots with slurs must be treated differently from those without. The pianist knows the difference between a *staccato*

and a *non-legato* which is longer than a pure *staccato*. The *non-legato* of the pianist (and Beethoven was one) more or less corresponds to the *portato* of the violinist. The pianist should note this *non-legato* in **bars 3, 5–6, 17–18**, and **25–26**, and the violinist in **bars 11, 13–14**, and **25–26**. It is regrettable that pianists as well as violinists put an *sfz* on the first note of the fourth bar of the theme. This note in *p* creates a contrast to the *espressivo* emphasis in the second bar. An inadvertent *crescendo* in **bars 5–7** for the pianist and **bars 13–15** for the violinist should be avoided.

In **bars 23–24** I would advise the pianist to execute the mordent relatively calmly, rather like this:

7

Variation I

Both partners are well advised to rehearse the first two bars of both the first and the second sections meticulously in order to achieve optimal unity of sound of these two heterogeneous instruments and to adjust them rhythmically to each other exactly. The violin is best practised with only the left hand of the piano:

8   9

In the first edition, in **bars 37–39**, we find that the *sfz*s of the violin are always on the last sixteenth-note, but in all other editions they conform with the *sfz* of the piano on the last but one. In Beethoven the self-willed dynamic of the first edition would be entirely credible. Unfortunately the autograph is missing.

Variation II

An audible change of position of the violin in the first or second bar and the (mostly unintentional) *glissando* it causes are æsthetically disturbing; one ought to strive for a perfectly clear definition of the run, as in the piano. Hence the following proposal for the fingering:

10

Musically speaking, a contrasting treatment of the two hands in the piano part of this variation is very attractive, that is, the right hand very *legato* with a slight stress on every top note, and in the left a kind of '*buffo*' *staccato*.

In **bar 60** of the piano part it is astonishing that in the first edition the *sfz* in the right hand is not on the first note, as it is in all other texts – presumably to conform with the violin part – but not until the third thirty-second-note:

11

A most attractive thought!

Variation III: *Minore*

Here both instrumentalists must take pains to avoid a *diminuendo* in **bars 72, 74, 76, 80, 82, 84, 87–88, 90, 92** and at the end of the variation, for the subsequent *piano subito*s give this variation its demonic character.

The apparently ludicrous dynamics in the piano, such as, for instance, on the upbeat to **bar 73** and **bar 89**, are in my opinion deliberate; unfortunately this is often played *piano*.

Joseph Szigeti proposes a *martelé* at the nut for the violinists,[3] which is possible but very personal, and can be replaced today by a hard *spiccato*, also near the nut.

Variation IV: *Maggiore*

The pianist should bring out somewhat the middle voice with its syncopated theme in the right hand rather more than the rest of the material. The dots in the violin part, in **bars 105–106, 113–114, 128–130** and **134**, are to be taken entirely seriously, just as in the piano in **bars 113–114** and **121–124**; and this holds true for **bars 129–133** as well as for the last triplet in **bar 135**.

From **bar 117** I recommend restraint in violin tone and in the right hand of the piano but not in the left.

Within the thematic material, which is split up between the two instruments in **bars 125–128**, I consider the entry of the violin correct only at the top note of the piano *arpeggio*, so that the theme can be taken over seamlessly.

Third Movement: *Rondo. Allegro*

The tempo indication of this movement, *Allegro*, without any of the customary additions (such as *assai, molto, vivace, con spirito, ma non troppo, con brio, moderato, ma non tanto*, and so on), gives cause for speculation as to the correct tempo. We find the same unqualified tempo indication also in the following

[3] *op. cit.*, p. 7.

Sonatas: No. 5, first movement; No. 6, first movement; No. 7, third and fourth movements; No. 10, third movement. Most good and experienced musicians can recognize instinctively the character and thus the tempo, and yet this movement is, to my mind, usually played slower than the music demands.

The absence of a shortening dot at every upbeat of the rondo theme in the piano as well as in the violin is worth mention. Is there purpose to it? My belief is that the upbeat should be short as well.

I consider quite justified the adjustment of some dynamic indications in parallel passages, even if the specifications in the two parts are different or are partly missing, as in **bars 17, 21, 23, 50–51, 93, 118–119, 135, 139, 141, 154–155, 162, 168–169, 184, 186, 196, 209** and **215**. In this last bar, there is in the first edition an *ff* for the sixteenth-note entry of the violin. It is clear that this sixteenth-note should also be played loudly the first time, in **bars 211–212**. But why an *ff*, which incidentally is missing in the piano part, is given only the second time I do not quite understand. This *ff* is eliminated in all other editions.

In spite of the absence of dynamic notation the pianist will surely keep the beginning of the movement and every repetition of the rondo theme in *p* – with the exception of **bars 127–134**. The same is true for the violin in **bars 8** and **59**. In all these cases an *f* follows later (**bars 17** and **127**), and in **bar 64** even with a *cresc.*

The dots above and below the notes of the violin part in this movement are, because of its character, taken almost throughout as *spiccato*. Here also a differentiation of the notation would be useful, such as I employ in all my editions, with the exception of Urtexts: dots alone indicate a short *martelé*, i.e. on the string. If the dot has a stroke ⁔ as well, then soft, elongated *martelé* bows are meant. But where there is a wedge ▼, a short *saltato* note is indicated, that is, off the string. With a stroke ▼̄ a *saltato* bowing is also intended, but softer and elongated. With this notation the violinist would not – at least, not in this respect – be groping in the dark.

The *sfz* in **bars 17** and **135** is to be considered as an *f*, if only because of the *piano subito* which follows two bars later.

For the *ff* in **bar 37** some restraint is essential, and I therefore recommend playing the *f* in **bars 31–36** only moderately loudly, as in the parallel passages in **bars 149–155**.

The violinist should interpret the upbeat in **bars 43** and **161** as such and not (as I have often heard) start the phrase only in the next bar. Possibly the player is led astray here because the *p* in most editions is specified only at the beginning of **bars 44** and **162** respectively.

I would advise the violinist to adjust the dynamics in **bars 50–51** to those of the piano. In the first edition, but also in some later publictions, the swell for the violin is not indicated until **bar 51**. In the first place, this notation does not correspond with that in the parallel passage in **bars 168–169**, where even in the first edition the swell begins already in the previous bar, and secondly, it is quite unlikely that the dynamics of the two instruments at this point should be different only the first time; thus not:

12 but: 13

It is odd that in the violin part in many editions the fourth eighth-note in **bar 73** is missing, although there can be no doubt about it; thus:

14 and not: 15

I believe that the *p sub.* in **bar 76** should be taken seriously by both instruments, although what one mostly hears is a *dim.* already in **bar 75**. The rests written for the violin in **bars 81–82** and **89–90** are of real importance for the animation, lightness and elegance of this theme and must by no means be overlooked, as, unfortunately, happens so often. In the violin part in **bar 93** a *pp* is obviously missing, and is rightly restored in some editions. **Bars 93–96** should not then be looked on as an accompaniment to the leading piano part; what we are dealing with here is a contrapuntal line set with warmth against the piano melodically, in order to repeat canonically from **bar 97** the previous four bars of the piano.

It would be a pity to dilute the *sfz*s in **bars 103–109** – quite significantly noted for the two instruments at different points – by mutual adaptation. In **bar 118** the violinist should – despite the absence of a *cresc.* – adjust to the piano. In **bar 119** the theme certainly must be continued *p* even after the *fp*, for from **bar 127** and its upbeat the piano has, in contrast to the *piano* presentation of the theme up to now, a real *f* for the first time. At this point Joseph Szigeti recommends[4] a curious fingering:

16

As in all things with this great master, something along these lines is undoubtedly interesting, but, to be honest, rather odd. Perhaps Szigeti arrived at such an idea because in days gone by all D strings were considerably weaker than the others, even on the finest instruments. The silver D string available today is now just as strong as the others, making such a concession superfluous.

I would recommend that the pianist wait a little in **bar 170** with his new entry after the *fermata*, first, to let the previous chord die away, and also to allow the violinist to enter with precision. In the violin figure in **bars 178–182** I play the first and the fourth eighth-notes each on a different string:

17

In the violin part of all editions the *cresc.* in **bar 186**, which (as in the piano part) leads to the climax in **bar 191**, is

[4] *ibid.*, p. 18.

missing. The dynamic contrasts from **bar 201** to the end are noted very precisely, and must also be followed precisely. In these works, obviously, Beethoven almost – but not quite – always spared no effort to give precise dynamic indications, sometimes hair-raising in their difficulty, but nonetheless an integral part of the composition itself. To ignore that – which unfortunately often happens – is tantamount to changing the actual text.

Sonata No. 2 in A major, Op. 12, No. 2

Dedicated to Antonio Salieri
Manuscript missing
Composed 1797–98
First edition end of 1798 or beginning of 1799

Introduction

This Sonata differs considerably in character from the First and Third Sonatas of Op. 12; both are more brimful of energy and more dramatic, while this one, No. 2, is still closely bound to the *galant* style. Although a truly charming work, it does not, unfortunately, enjoy general popularity. It may be that the violinist of today, more inclined to a soloistic style, finds he has 'too little to do' in this Second Sonata and is often confined to playing accompanying figuration. Incidentally, it is peculiar that the odd-numbered Sonatas, Nos. 1, 3, 5, 7 and 9, are to be heard a good deal more often in concert than the others – a preference I do not share.

First Movement: *Allegro vivace*

As the main theme of the first movement should be presented as essentially graceful, I would recommend that both partners always shorten the second eighth-note.

Ensemble can be gravely endangered when runs are not executed precisely according to the rhythm (**bars 9–10** in the piano and **bars 13–14** in the violin). Similar passages can be found in **bars 25–26**, **96–97**, **132–133**, and **136–137**.

The violinist will find it helpful to split his bowings in **bars 13–14**, **25–26**, and **136–137**; otherwise he will be in danger

ant. Salieri
nat. a Legnago 19 Ag.
1750

Tr. Rehberg ad viv del
Vienna 6 Febr. 1821

Antonio Salieri
18 August 1750–7 May 1825

Italian composer and, after Joseph Haydn, Johann Schenk and Johann Georg Albrechtsberger, Beethoven's fourth composition teacher. Salieri's relationship with Mozart is still the subject of heated debate, and the rumour that Salieri poisoned him recurs intermittently, stimulated by such over-interpretations of Salieri's hostility to Mozart as Pushkin's 1830 poem and Rimsky-Korsakov's opera *Mozart and Salieri* based on it and, most recently, Peter Shaffer's play, *Amadeus*. Salieri's other composition pupils included Schubert and Liszt, and his own compositions include more than 40 operas, church music and many vocal and instrumental pieces. He was declared mentally deranged in 1823.

of being so overshadowed by the *f* passages in the piano part that his runs are hardly audible. Naturally, this presupposes (as in all similar cases) an inaudible bow change which produces no acoustic difference from the original phrasing. In the *p* run in **bars 96–97** a bow change is unnecessary.

In **bar 30** the violinist should begin the *p* only on the second eighth-note and not (as in the first edition) on the first eighth. From the point of view of musical phrasing as well as that of acoustics, a *p* in the violin at the beginning of the bar would be not only unreasonable but also inaudible, as in the piano part the *f* is carried though to the end of the phrase, and hence logically also to the first part of the bar. The situation is similar in **bars 36** and **152**.

In **bars 34–35** and **150–151** both instruments often, incorrectly, play *piano* after the *sfz*. In my opinion the *cresc.* in **bars 32**, and also **148**, continues up to the *p sub.* in **bar 36** and, in the second case, to **bar 152**; and so the *sfz*s do not interrupt the *cresc.*

The dots in **bars 31–35** and **146–151** should not be played too short by the violinist, but rather in a singing style – which applies also to the piano part in **bars 36–41** and **152–157**.

The dot on the quarter-note in this figure

18

should undoubtedly be interpreted by the piano as well as the violin (**bars 46–54** and **162–170**) as a shortening of the quarter-note. Hence my (by now familiar) marking ⌐ signifies a rest *before* the last note, and ⌐ means a rest *after* the last note, i.e., a shortening of its value. But this is an orthographic difference that, unfortunately, I have not found in any edition.

The rather wilful dynamic in **bars 58** and **174**, noted differently for the two instruments, seems to me appropriate, since for the violin the phrase does indeed begin at the beginning of the bar, but for the piano only from the second half of the bar.

The *sfz* in **bars 48–53** and **164–169** should be interpreted both for violin and piano as within the *piano* phrase; it should not, as so often happens with Beethoven, be equated with an *f*.

The piano interjections in **bars 62–63** and **178–179** must not be performed too quietly, so that the difference from the following *pp* becomes clearly noticeable; this applies also to the violin in **bars 63** and **179**.

An especially precise execution of the phrasing in the piano, as in the violin, is required in **bars 68–83** and **184–199**, for the articulation changes in **bars 74–75**, **81–83** and also in **bars 190–191** and **197–199**:

There should thus be no *staccato* on the last eighth-note of **bars 70**, **72**, **73**, **78**, **80** and **82** any more than on **186**, **188**, **194** and **196**. In contrast, the dot over the second half of **bars 74**, **75**, and **81–83**, as also **190**, **191**, and **197–199**, must be strictly observed, i.e., shortened:

The last eighth-note of **bars 74**, **75**, and **81–85** as well as **190**, **191**, and **197–201** are undoubtedly short *staccato* notes.

The beginning of the second part, in **bar 88**, remains problematic for the piano. In the first edition the *acciaccatura* is noted thus:

In the Henle Urtext edition it is given erroneously as:

i.e., not shortened. In other older editions, as in that by Joseph Joachim, it is even written out as eighth-notes:

Both first and third versions (Exx. 20 and 22) are conceivable;
I prefer the short *acciaccatura* in this case, especially as the
corresponding eighth-notes for the violin are written out.

The absence of the *sfz* in the violin part in the second half of
bars 103 and **105** (in contrast to the piano in **bars 104** and
106) is entirely justified and should be respected, not 'im-
proved' – the more so in that in both instruments the *sfz*s in
bars 107–108 are treated alike.

The differing dynamic markings for the two instruments at
the beginning of the recapitulation (**bar 124**) I find uncon-
vincing. Although even in the first edition the notation *fp* in
the piano and *p* in the violin is already given at the beginning
of the bar, the violin and piano parts were not then printed as
an integral score but separately, and this discrepancy probably went unnoticed by engraver and composer. I would
follow the marking in the piano part and also play an *fp*.

The notation of **bar 161** of the violin in the first printing is
odd:

23

but I agree with most editors in arranging this bar just like
bar 45:

24

but I agree with most editors in arranging this bar just like

With the change in rhythm for the violin in **bar 216**, the
direction of the bow stroke should also be changed. My
proposal: **bars 212–215** always in upbows (V), as they
should still be played *p* and gracefully, but to change to
downbows (⊓) for **bars 216–220**, the better to illustrate the
increasing breathless excitement.

Pianists often neglect the *p sub.* in **bar 226**; they either
introduce a *diminuendo* beforehand, in the run, or play the first
note of the bar as an *fp*.

The technical execution of the left hand in the piano in **bars**

242–244 often leaves something to be desired, because the octaves mostly do not sound *legato*.

To this movement I would like to add a little anecdote. At one of my performances of this Sonata a very well-known Viennese musician of the older generation, who must remain nameless, was present. He found the interpretation on the whole satisfactory, but in his opinion the first movement should have been taken much slower, something like a really *gemütlich* Viennese waltz, perhaps even with the traditional premature second eighth-note!

Second Movement: *Andante più tosto Allegretto*

In Beethoven we sometimes find markings for the movements which not everybody understands. I find it incomprehensible that so many students (but not only they) feel no need to fathom such detailed indications from a composer. I have, for instance, met but few violinists who gave any real consideration to what Mozart meant by the unusual marking *aperto* in the first movement of his A major Violin Concerto, K.219.

At the head of the second movement of the Sonata with which we are now dealing we read *Andante più tosto Allegretto*, a marking for which very few musicians take the trouble to account. As I mentioned in my introduction to this Sonata, the character of the work is in more of a *galant* style, and so, too, with this movement; it will, therefore, be helpful to understand the marking of this movement. One possible paraphrase is: '*Andante*, almost like an *allegretto*', and thus it is an important hint not to interpret the movement tragically nor to take it too slowly. The contrasting phrasing of the main theme in the piano and in the violin is here, for once, to be understood as a bowing instruction for the violin. In **bar 111** the piano suddenly has a different phrasing. I do not consider this an intentional variant. In the third bar of this phrase the pianist is again confronted with a problem: there should actually be a *crescendo* on the first quarter-note, which on the violin can be attained easily and well. Unfortunately this is not possible for the pianist, and a deep, often audible, groan or intake of breath is no substitute! All he can do is just play the second quarter-note louder than the first; this applies equally to **bars 11**, **18**, **26**, **71**, **80**, **86**, **113** and **115**. Similarly in the dynamics one should not try to avoid making delicate nuances. The first chord is often played similarly to that of **bar 5**, i.e., with an *fp*, but at the beginning it must be strictly *p*.

In **bar 6** the first eighth-note is tied to the previous sixteenth-notes but is shortened by the dot. These shortenings are to be executed correspondingly everywhere where the closing note has a dot. In my orthography it looks like this:⌣. or ⌢ not inside the slur.

As already mentioned, I would mark **bar 6** as follows:

25

The last three notes are to be understood as *non-legato*, i.e., not too short. The sudden *pp* in **bar 7** I consider very important; accordingly the previous *p* must not be too quiet. Exactly the same holds true of the playing of the main theme in the violin in **bars 9–16**. For the violinist I should like once more to stress: don't play too short in **bar 14**, for the notation in the piano part means *non-legato* when there is a slur above or below the dots.

Before **bars 20**, **28**, **88** and **96** I propose a slight hesitation to give the last *sfz* more emphasis than the previous ones. The violin must therefore also delay the second sixteenth-note in **bar 88**, as must the piano in **bar 96**.

The violin leads in **bars 33–40**; accordingly the piano plays the canon in imitation and a little more quietly. While the violin in the last bar of this phrase (**bar 40**) rather decreases in volume, the piano intensifies to the point where it takes the lead in this secondary theme, starting with **bar 41**. Here the violinist proceeds with the canon (**bars 42–48**) just as the piano did previously; he leaves the leadership to the piano. Though not expressly demanded, the dynamic in the second subject, **bars 33–48**, amounts to a slight *crescendo* towards the second, fourth and sixth bars which seems to me natural and entirely appropriate:

26

The second part of the canon begins with the upbeat of the violin to **bar 49** and again the violin dominates, up to **bar 56**. From this bar on the piano takes the leadership.

I find the dynamic marking (or rather the absence of precise dynamic indications) in **bars 79–83** a little confusing. I must assume that the piano from the second sixteenth-note of the octaves in **bar 79** on has to be in *p*, similar to **bar 71** of the violin, otherwise the *p* in the violin would make no sense. My assumption of a missing *p* in **bar 79** of the piano part is all the more plausible, as otherwise the *f* marked in **bar 81** would be superfluous. The *sfz* in the violin in **bar 81** should, as so often in Beethoven, be understood as *f*, for otherwise there would be no reason for the *p* in **bar 83**, where, incidentally, the *p* is also missing in the piano part.

As the piano begins the *cresc.* already at the beginning of **bar 109**, I would advise the violinist to enter with the same dynamic volume that the piano has reached.

The precisely noted dynamics from **bar 111** to the end of the movement are to be followed meticulously, as, for instance, the *p* (and not *pp*) in **bar 115**, which is not followed by the *pp* until **bar 119**. **Bar 120** closes the previous phrase on the first sixteenth-note of the violin, and the new one begins with the second sixteenth-note in a way similar to **bars 121** and **124** in the piano part. This does not indicate a separation of the first sixteenth-note from the second one, but a tiny lengthening of the first note with a slight dynamic support, something like this:

27

It is also interesting to compare the dynamics in **bar 124** of the piano where the *cresc.* does not start until the second sixteenth-note. The penultimate bar is, after the previous *rinf.*, a genuine *p sub.* – but must not yet be a *pp*, which is reserved for the last two beats.

Let me repeat that the interpretation of this whole movement should not be conceived dramatically: the *galant* style nowhere transgresses the limits of good manners, and it is thus advisable to play with a refined, beautiful and elegant production of tone.

Third Movement: *Allegro piacevole*

Here, too, the tempo indication of the movement is unusual. To players who aren't sure what Beethoven meant by *piacevole* I usually explain it as 'pleasantly', 'agreeably', 'engagingly' – and it is a further pointer to the serene and charming character of the Sonata as a whole.

In this rondo one finds that, in contrast to the first bar, a shortening dot on the second quarter-note in the second and third bars is conspicuously absent. I am sure this is no oversight because we find differentiated treatment in the two parts thoughout the whole movement. The execution should therefore sound something like this:

28

for both piano and violin.

Beethoven's typical rough humour is evident again in so-called 'wrong' accents in **bars 34–48** and in the parallel passage in **bars 263–277**. In **bar 33** as in **bar 262** in the piano part an *f* is missing which, in view of what follows, is imperative here. The hint given by the *p* in **bars 38** and **267** in the piano part is further proof. In **bar 49** a *p* is missing although it is present in the equivalent **bar 278**. The shading from *p* to *pp* in **bars 51–53** and at the same place in the recapitulation (**bars 280–282**) should be observed carefully, for it introduces the delicate and calm second subject.

The *p* of **bars 61** and **65**, given in brackets in some editions, quite properly follows the *p* of the first edition (**bars 290** and **294** of the violin part).

In **bars 72–82** the shortening of the last quarter-note in each case in both instruments should be observed scrupulously; this is repeated in the recapitulation, in **bars 301–311**. The pianist should shape his **bars 116–119**, a third lower than the violin, in such a way that the higher voice of the violin is clearly recognizable, and all the more so as the new thematic material is carried on by the violin in the following sixteen bars. The left hand in the piano could lovingly imitate the *espressivo* of a cello to the accompanying right hand. With the upbeat at the second eighth-note (**bar 135**) the pianist can prepare the intensification towards the subsequent piano theme by a slight *cresc.* And the violin should not play over-sensitively in **bars 136–151**: we do not have here a pure accompaniment, for the passage has a contrapuntal character. To make clear the amiable calm in **bar 132**, **bars 128–131** ought to be charged with tension, which, of course, is true also of **bars 144–148**.

With the last two quarter-notes in **bar 151** the violin again takes up the second part of the theme; the relationship of the volume of the accompanying right hand in the piano as well as the expressive left hand should be adjusted to **bars 120–134**. **Bars 167–183** should be treated similarly to the earlier **bars 151–167**.

In the first edition the violin part in **bar 180** reads:

29

According to this, the penultimate eighth-note is a C, and not (as in many other early editions) a C sharp. The C natural of the first edition and of the modern Urtext editions does not convince me; although both versions seem possible, I prefer – perhaps from habit – the C sharp.

The rather complicated dynamic in **bars 184–231** must be

scrupulously observed: first, a *cresc.* over four bars, followed by a *decresc.* also over four bars. A real *pp* is required in **bar 192** to permit a definitely stronger *p* in the following bar, if only because a *decresc.* follows.

Bar 198 is also *p* and therefore must be played louder than **bar 200**. A steep *crescendo* follows, virtually from nothing, from *pp* to *ff* over only four bars which – when performed correctly – has an extraordinarily dramatic effect.

The gradation from *p* in the second quarter-note of **bar 216** to the *pp* in **bar 226** is also very attractive; it would be regrettable if it were overlooked. The opposing dynamics in the piano and violin in **bars 328–329** are surely intentional and in keeping with an idea logically realized. But the thematic entry of the violin in the joint playing of the *f* of the piano and the *p* of the violin would not be audible. With due regard to the correct basic idea, this problem must be solved by the best compromise that is acoustically acceptable.

Not everything in music needs to be philosophical, dramatic or deeply serious. Gaiety, light-heartedness and youthful freshness have their place, too, and anyone who recognizes and enjoys the lovely, unburdened character of this Sonata and can perform it accordingly will do justice to this charming work.

Sonata No. 3 in E flat major, Op. 12, No. 3

Dedicated to Antonio Salieri
Manuscript missing
Composed 1797–98
First edition end of 1798 or beginning of 1799

Introduction

Of the first three Violin Sonatas I consider this the most dramatic, although not to the same extent as, for instance, the A minor Sonata, Op. 23, the C minor Sonata, Op. 30, No. 2 or the *Kreutzer* Sonata, Op. 47; but the slow second movement does give us a presentiment of the late Beethoven.

The first movement is especially dreaded by pianists, for the runs in the desired tempo are not at all easy, and considerably more difficult than for the violinist. The first and third movements are, in a similar manner to the first two Sonatas, still youthfully carefree, even playful here and there, if not with quite as rough a sense of humour as Beethoven could show in other works.

The attempt to realize faithfully the prescribed dynamics confronts the two partners with considerable problems, especially in the last movement. They can definitely be mastered – and it is certainly worth the effort!

First Movement: *Allegro con spirito*

The upbeats, first in the piano and then in both instruments, in **bars 2** and **4** are often played *f* or are provided with a *cresc.*; the same occurs in the recapitulation in **bars 105** and **107**. Let me state clearly here that the difference in dynamics in the

Ignaz Schuppanzigh
20 November 1776–2 March 1830

Austrian violinist and leader of his famous eponymous string
quartet, which gave the premieres of many Beethoven quartets. In
his first few years in Vienna Beethoven was a violin pupil of Schuppanzigh, and over the years a close friendship developed between
the two men. Schuppanzigh must have been the butt of much of
Beethoven's coarse humour; indeed, Beethoven's conversation
books and correspondence occasionally refer to him as 'Milord
Falstaffs'. The bars which follow are the beginning of a composition
by Beethoven (WoO 100) entitled *Lob auf den Dicken – Praise to the Fat
One*, for three solo voices and chorus, of 1801:

Schup- pan-zigh ist ein Lump, Lump, Lump
(Schup- pan-zigh is an oaf, oaf, oaf)

piano at the beginning of the exposition (**bars 1–4**) and in the recapitulation (**bars 104–107**) is certainly intentional, a fact unfortunately often neglected. The upbeat of the violin to **bar 5** can begin with a slight delay, so that the first four bars seem a kind of 'prelude', as it were; and likewise with **bar 107**. The dots which here too are specified by Beethoven for both instruments

would be clearer in my version: when a note is to be shortened I put the dot outside the slur:

The eighth-note is thus to be understood as a sixteenth-note. Do not develop the *cresc.* in **bar 9** too quickly, so that the climax is not reached already in **bar 11** – which was not the composer's intention.

Whether in **bars 13** and **115** a *p sub.* is to be played on the first beat is a moot point, as the *p* in the violin part in the first edition is placed between the first and the second eighth-notes in **bar 13** and is missing completely in **bar 115**. In the piano part the *p* is indeed placed at the beginning of the bar in both places, and it is therefore more appropriate to play the *p* in both instruments on the first beat. As so often in Beethoven, the *sfz* in the violin part (**bar 18**) is to be understood as *f*, in accordance with the piano part. The *cresc.* in **bar 21** leads eventually to the *ff* in **bar 22** and marks an even stronger intensification.

The dynamics of **bar 23** are quite obscure. In the violin part the *acciaccatura* on A could still be *ff*, and the *p sub.* not until the main note, F. Furthermore, in the piano part too the *p* is not to be employed until the second eighth-note or even (as in the first edition) on the fourth quarter-note. For the beginning of **bar 23** the *ff* is in any case obligatory for both instruments. In the phrasing of the violin, in **bars 30** and **126** it would seem that a slight shortening of the third quarter-note is required so that the trill on the fourth quarter-note has the effect of an upbeat. The grace-note in **bar 30** (which incidentally is missing in the parallel spot in the first edition in **bar 126**) must of course be supplied and tied to the trill.

The left hand of the piano in **bars 29–36** and **125–132** should not be regarded merely as a purely bass figure; an *espressivo* as a counterpart to the violin part is particularly attractive. **Bars 31** and **127** in the violin, as **39** and **135** in the piano, are not to be understood as short notes; dots with slurs should be interpreted as *non-legato*.

Many violinists find Beethoven's instructions for phrasing in **bars 33** and **129** unclear and therefore execute them quite differently. In the first edition and in the Urtext editions one finds

32

but in the next bar

33

Even more confusing are the corresponding instructions in the piano part in **bar 41**

34

and **bar 137**

35

It is certain that **bars 33–34** and **129** should be phrased differently from the following ones. But how? My proposal is to adopt the phrasing of the violin in **bar 36** for both instruments in all analogous places in this movement:

In many performances the dots in the violin part, in **bars 37–43** and **133–139**, are construed to mean spring bows. In my opinion this is an error, for two reasons: first, the realization is already usually unsatisfactory because of the unavoidable string-crossing, and secondly, dots are often used as *non-legato* by many composers.

The entry of the violin, in **bars 45** and **141**, should not start as a true *p* but already at the dynamic level the piano has reached through the *cresc.* of **bars 44** and **140** respectively. One should also take care that the *f* in **bars 47** and **143** allows of a further increase to the *ff* in **bars 49** and **145**. The length of the eighth-notes in **bars 50–51** and **146–147** should be mutually adjusted in the two instruments.

In **bar 58** of the piano part the *p* on the second eighth-note is missing; it should be taken into account just as in **bar 154**. Also in the piano in **bars 59–63** the dots above the last eighth-notes are missing

which Beethoven writes out in the parallel passage in **bars 155–159**.

In the left hand of the piano, too, some dots are missing in many editions. At the beginning of **bars 89–95** dots should be inserted, but in the last three bars towards the lyrical C flat major modulation a transition through gradual lengthening is appropriate. The dynamic shading from the *p* to the *pp* in the piano, in **bars 62** and **158**, on the sixth eighth-note and in the violin, in **bars 63** and **159**, is desirable. Nor should the differentiation from the *f* in **bars 64** and **160** to the *ff* in **bars 66** and **162** be neglected. The chords in **bars 68–74** are often ripped off all too abruptly in the violin as well as in the left hand of the piano. They are, after all, quarter-notes without shortening dots and should not be played like the shortened eighth-notes in the right hand of the piano. The violinist should not be afraid of splitting bowings in the passages in **bars 75** and **77**, for he is playing in the less brilliant middle range – but he really should produce a genuine *ff*. The *sfz* for the two instruments in **bars 82–83**, **86–87**, and **90–91** should be interpreted as an *fp*. This is one of Beethoven's contradictions and an example of the *occasional* inaccuracy of his dynamic markings. But that's what we interpreters are for! In the enchanting C flat major passage from **bar 96** the mordent in **bar 98** should, in my opinion, be played by the violinist as well, though it is not so noted in the first edition nor in some later ones. Rhythmicly, it should be played very calmly, rather as:

38

In the coda the dynamic in **bar 165** is executed inexactly by most violinists; in such cases either the whole passage remains *f*, or the *p* is already reached by the second half of the bar. It seems advisable to me to play the shortened quarter-notes of the piano in **bar 168** and of the violin in the next bar in a singing manner and not at all too short, so as to make a clear contrast with the following eighth-notes of **bars 170** and **171**. A *ritardando* in the last bar is not advisable.

Second Movement: *Adagio con molta espressione*

At the beginning of this movement the accompanying eighth-notes in the violin and in the left hand of the piano should be held for their full lengths, unshortened and calmly, as should the *non-legato* in **bars 4** and **6**.

Fanatics of the Urtext will doubtless assume that **bar 6** in the violin part should not be executed analogously to the piano's **bar 4** because of the absence of the dots and the slur! The mordent in **bar 2** of the piano and **bar 10** of the violin is often performed as follows:

39

which the composer could have written without difficulty. This execution seems to me somewhat pedantic and clumsy, and I therefore propose, as in many similar cases, to relax the rhythm a little, rather like this:

40

The habit of many instrumentalists to carry over baroque principles into later stylistic periods seems to me questionable, at the least. Thus the mordents in the piano in **bars 4, 6, 42**, and **44** as well as in the violin in **bar 12** are often commenced with the upper auxiliary note:

41

The ascending line, free from ornament, is without a doubt:

42

and the E on the penultimate note should therefore not be anticipated. My proposal is:

43

The pianist should be aware of the difference of the ornament in **bars 4** and **6** as well as in **bars 42** and **44**, i.e., with an additional trill the second time.

In **bar 8** the violin gradually changes from its initial accompanying figure to being the main exponent of the theme; this can best be made clear by a slight *crescendo*. The bass figure in the left hand of the piano in **bars 9–14** is often not presented in the typical Beethovenian style. (Artur Schnabel was an outstanding interpreter of such secondary figures which, in his hands, strikingly revealed their intrinsic significance.) One should attend to this passage with special love and care. The grace-note at the beginning of **bar 15** in the violin is performed differently by various interpreters: in some performances I have heard a very short grace-note and in others a long one with the value of a full eighth-note. Personally, I prefer a calm sixteenth-note:

44

It remains unclear whether the grace-note in **bar 19** in the piano part should still be *f* or already *p*. The dynamic marking, especially in the violin part, could be an indication that the *p* should not start until the main note. As one cannot be sure that the earliest editions give the dynamic indications at exactly the right positions, it is possible here to start the *p* in the violin – as with the piano – at the beginning of the bar. **Bars 35** and **36** should in each case be started quietly, after the *sfz* on the last quarter-note of the preceding bar. I recommend that the violinist prolong the last eighth-note a little in **bar 38** so that the first note of the next bar does not coincide with the grace-note of the piano but is not played until the main note.

The *cresc.* in **bar 42** requires the concurrence of the violin, although the actual notation is missing, for the *p* in **bar 43** should certainly be understood as *subito*, which is clearly evident from the dynamic of the piano. And the same applies to **bar 44**.

The grace-notes in **bar 45** of the piano should in my opinion be anticipated, that is, played rhythmically before the main notes of the bar. The mordent in **bar 48** is not infrequently performed without much thought. My proposal is:

45

so that the last thirty-second-note coincides exactly with the upbeat of the violin. The gradation *p* in **bar 50** and *pp* in **bars 51** and **57–58** should be taken more seriously than is commonly the case.

In **bar 52** of the violin part the mordent should not be:

46 but: 47

as stated above.

In the violin part in **bar 62** a *cresc.* is missing: this should lead to the *sfz* of the next bar, as with the dynamics in the piano part. To adapt the penultimate bar of the violin to the $\searrow$ of the piano part would not be good policy because the *p sub.* in the last bar is certainly intentional.

Third Movement: *Rondo. Allegro molto*

As well as the prescribed *sfz* in **bars 1** and **2**, some interpreters also play an *sfz* at the beginning of **bar 3** (and likewise **bar 7**), which is surely unintentional and avoidable. The violinist should not fall into the same error when playing the theme. This dynamic must be carefully observed in the rondo theme every time, although we find an exception in **bars 163–164** in the piano, where the *sfz*s are omitted in the first four bars. In **bars 16–17** and **174–175** the pianist does not always succeed in really shaping the sixteenth-notes of the right hand into pairs, which in the same figure in **bars 20–21** and **178–179** poses no particular difficulty for the violinist. A slight shortening of the second sixteenth-note can be helpful here.

The *sfz*s in **bars 24**, **26**, **28** and **30** are to be considered as within the context of the current *p*, for the following *cresc.* in **bar 31** would otherwise make no sense. Incidentally this *cresc.* should not be halted at the first *sfz* but develops from **bar 31** to the *ff* in **bar 40**. One should also avoid playing the last two eighth-notes of **bars 43**, **47**, **182**, **186** and **190** already in *f* which, unfortunately, often happens through simple inattentiveness; the following *ff* or *f* should in any case, enter without any preparation. The secondary theme, in **bar 52**, with upbeat could be played a tiny bit slower than the basic tempo of the movement. The shortening of the quarter-notes in **bars 72–75** is intentional, but there must be agreement between

violinist and pianist about the actual length. The dynamics of
the descending passage in the piano in **bars 75–78** are often
performed very imprecisely: either it stays in *f* up to the entry
of the violin or the *decresc.* occurs already in the second bar.
Beethoven brings a pleasing variant in the left hand in **bars
83–84**, through the *legato* which in other places is written as a
staccato. Although the accompanying figure in the violin in
bars 87–93 as well as **163–196** has no dots, I favour a light,
jumpy bow (*sautillé*) in order to rule out any ponderousness.

Bars 97, **101**, and **105–107** of the violin are very attractive
in *martelé* (i.e., short, on the string), in keeping with the rather
decisive character of this passage, and contrasts, moreover,
with a soft *spiccato* of **bars 109–116**.

I deal in the same way with **bars 117–129** (*martelé*) and,
correspondingly, **bars 131–146** (*spiccato*). To prepare for, or
return to, the rondo theme one might use a tiny delay in **bar
162**. The entry of the pedal note in the piano in **bar 245**
should, in my opinion, bring a sort of *pesante*, that is, it should
be very strong and somewhat slower.

With the upbeat to **bar 259** one should return to the old
tempo, light and elegant, but also with the eighth-notes short,
even in the left hand of the piano.

The change of character which occurs with **bar 266** is
noteworthy. Here all eighth-notes in violin and piano should
suddenly become softer and longer than before, and the
half-notes in the bass of the piano long and singing. An
evocation of farewell is already beginning. All the livelier and
shorter, almost *scherzando*, the last bars from **274** then follow.

Sonata No. 4 in A minor, Op. 23

Dedicated to Count Moritz von Fries
Manuscript missing
Composed 1800–01,
together with the Piano Sonata, Op. 22,
and the Sonata for Piano and Violin, Op. 24
First edition October 1801, together with Op. 24

Introduction

For the first time in the series of the Sonatas for piano and violin (with the exception of the second movement), the true dramatic power of Beethoven is here made manifest, far removed from the *galant* style used up till now. The breathlessness and tension in the outer movements already show signs of that development which reaches its highest point in this medium in the *Kreutzer* Sonata. It is incomprehensible that this work, too, is not heard more often in concert halls.

First Movement: *Presto*

The performance should make it clearly audible that in the first eight bars the piano is leading; the violin, despite its strong *sfz*, plays a secondary role. The upbeat in **bar 8** then gives the lead to the violin, which both players should make plain in character as well as in dynamic. There are differences between a leading thematic *piano*, a contrapuntal one, and finally an accompanying one. These three *piani* thus have different functions and can indeed differ from one another in essence. The violin remains more or less in the lead up to **bar 24**, and both instruments must effect clearly marked distinctions between *f* and *p*.

The piano does not take the lead until the second eighth-note of **bar 24**, despite the slur. One should compare here the phrasings, in **bar 26**, of the two instruments which should be understood as afterbeats. The violin enters the bar in the leading role, and in spite of the imitation it remains dominant up to the upbeat of the piano in **bar 37**.

Now the main voice should be continued in the piano up to **bar 54**. Here the violin takes over the principal part again for four bars, and is then superseded by the piano in *ff* – phrased differently – in **bar 58**.

I also think it important to clarify **bars 62–68**: the right hand of the piano has the upper voice from the second eighth-note of **bar 62**, and the violin again from the second eighth-note of **bar 64**. The second part, from **bar 76** up to the *p sub.* in **bar 84**, should be performed by the two instrumentalists in a hard, rhythmic, short, and uncompromising *ff*. With the exception of the descending line of the left hand of the piano in **bars 84**, **86**, **88**, and **90–94**, the violin remains in the lead. The *sfz*s noted in the violin and piano at different points must be heeded exactly.

The basic dynamic level actually remains p here up to the *cresc.* in **bar 108**. One might doubt the authenticity of the *fp* in the violin part on the second eighth-note of **bar 120**; it is, at least, odd. I believe it an error, and think it would be more logical with the piano on the first eighth-note. In any case the violin has the upper voice for two bars, and is superseded by the piano in **bar 122** at the second eighth-note. Although it is not noted, **bars 132–135** demand a *ritardando*, which, musically, is compelling and natural.

It is astonishing how often the secondary theme, which begins in **bar 136** with the preceding upbeat, is wrongly phrased by most players. Usually, from the second bar on they simply accentuate every half-bar, but the last eighth-note in the second and third bars must always be regarded as an upbeat. The only convincing phrasing seems to me something like the following:

48

It should be treated like this whenever this figure appears, and by both instruments. In the recapitulation I should especially like to point out that the dynamic is of a different kind from that of the beginning.

The rondo theme in the last movement of the Violin Concerto, Op. 61, poses a similar problem. Here, too, most violinists stress every half-bar, something like this:

49

instead of phrasing in conformity to the rhythmic formation of the accompaniment:

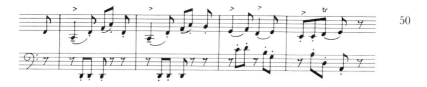

50

that is, the first, second, and fourth bars should be phrased as whole bars, but the third in half-bars; thus the stress in the first, second, and fourth bars lies on the first note, but in the third bar on the first as well as the fourth eighth-note.

In **bar 176** the violin continues in the lead from the second eighth-note as well, until the piano, in repetition and imitation, takes up the same figure from the second eighth-note of **bar 178**. Apart from that the recommendations for the exposition apply up to the coda.

Here I should like to mention again my proposals for phrasing. A slight delay of the entry of the violin at the beginning of the coda on the last eighth-note of **bar 223**, for reasons of character and acoustics, achieves the required calm after the previous stormy *ff*. The *p*s in **bars 239** and **241** are to be observed as genuinely *subito*, but should not be imitated in **bars 242–243**. The last three bars must be dynamically very clearly graded; thus the *p* in **bar 250** should not yet be played too quietly so that in the last bar a *pp* is still possible.

Second Movement: *Andante scherzoso più Allegretto*

Throughout this movement, the dot on each slurred eighth-note, whether noted or not, should always be understood as a shortening:

51

The upbeat to the *fugato*, in **bars 32**, **36**, **39** and **42**, as in **91–93** and **159** and **162**, should not be interpreted as a short *staccato* note, even if two bars later the last two eighth-notes are provided with dots. I understand the phrasing in the following way:

52

This holds true for both instruments.

The different *sfz*s in the two instruments, in **bars 60** and **62–64**, and **180** and **182–184**, are here, except for the important accents, meant as sustained *f*s, for otherwise the *p* notation in **bars 61, 65, 181** and **185** would be meaningless. (Incidentally, in **bar 185** the *p* is missing and should be supplied as in **bar 65**.)

From the second half of **bar 68** up to the second half of **bar 72** the violin has the upper voice, then the piano leads in a rhythmically varied way in sixteenth-note octaves.

The two eighth-notes with dots in **bars 77, 79, 81, 83** as well as **197, 199, 201** and **203** should be executed broadly, not only because of the *non-legato* notation in the piano part with a slur over the dots, but also to do justice to the soft, singing character. The two long octave A's in the violin in **bars 123–125** and **127–129** are difficult to realize because of the problem of bow division. Some violinists divide the stroke in both cases, which does not provide an ideal solution. Whether upbow or downbow is not important, but an uneven bow division is absolutely necessary. One should therefore save bow at the beginning and increase the speed of the bow during the stroke, so that the *crescendo* intended can be realized. The grace-note, missing after the trill in the piano in **bar 137**, should be supplied as in **bar 133**.

Bars 46–50 and **166–170** must be performed as blocks of one bar each, without dynamic transitions: no *dim.* to the *p* or *cresc.* to the *f*.

Third Movement: *Allegro molto*

Although the tempo of this movement is in half-bars and is also rather fast, one should beware of playing this movement *presto*. The tension and breathlessness in its character can be achieved by means other than mere speed.

In **bars 1–8** all notes in the violin part should be slightly separated, so that too smooth a bow change does not spoil the rhythmic definition. In **bar 7** *staccato* dots for the violin as well as for the left hand of the piano seem to me to be indispensible.

Here a comparison with the original dotted notation in the violin part in **bar 15** is useful. In this bar, too, the notes in the left hand of the piano should be short (see also the piano part in **bars 318** and **322**).

One should heed the exact dynamic notation in the rondo theme in **bar 6**: after the *sfz*, immediately *dim.* to the *p* of the next bar, and in the same way in **bar 14** – unlike **bars 18–20, 71–73, 111–113, 221–223** and **317–323**.

I understand the phrasing in **bars 20–24** of the piano like this:

53

by which I do not mean an alteration of the rhythm.

At the last quarter-note of **bar 35** in the violin part the leading upper voice should be observed up to the third quarter-note of **bar 39**, after which the piano takes over the lead up to the first quarter-note of **bar 43**. It is true that in this bar a *p sub.* is written for both parts; but with the following *decresc.* in mind, one must not play *pp* immediately. The different dynamic notation for the two instruments in **bar 49** does not seem justified to me. The *p* in the violin is indeed adjusted to **bar 51** of the piano, but it is unrealistic as far as the balance is concerned. I thus believe that before the noted *p* an *f* has simply been overlooked.

For the rhythmic distribution of the seven small notes for the violin in **bar 51** and the piano in **bar 53** the two partners should come to an agreement so that the two instruments do not phrase differently. My proposal is:

54

The rhythm in the intermezzo, in **bars 74–93**, is rather difficult. Between the first two quarter-notes of the piano and the third and fourth of the violin no unevenness should be shown, and certainly no *rubato*. It is imperative that the rhythm be strictly adhered to! And I should mention, incidentally, that **bars 88−89** and **92−93** show substantial lengthenings in comparison to **bar 81**.

In the subsidiary theme, in **bars 113−203**, I consider grace-notes advisable for all trills, although not expressly prescribed by Beethoven. (Compare **bar 282**, where Beethoven writes out such grace-notes specifically.) For instance, in **bars 120** and **152** of the violin:

 55

And in the piano part in **bars 128**, **144**, **160** and **176**:

56

In **bars 191–195**:

 57

All the *p sub*.s noted in **bars 129**, **137**, **145**, **153**, **161**, **169**, and **177** should be observed most faithfully, for they are the living expression of the intended tension.

At the same time one must always be careful not to confuse *p* and *pp*, as the example in **bars 177–178** shows. The slurred notes in **bars 198−201** should not be played too short, despite the dots above the quarter-notes, since they again present the pianistic notation of *non-legato*. The chords in the violin in **bars 223–231** must not be spread, for this would falsify the dramatic and rhythmic character of this passage; and besides it would not occur to any pianist to arpeggiate his chords here.

The following fingerings offers violinistic refinement which, through the choice of the E string for the *sfz*, puts the dynamic almost automatically in the right perspective (**bars 235–245**):

In **bars 259–266** the same distribution of upper and lower voices is to be used as in **bars 35–43**, i.e., the violin leads from the last quarter-note of **bar 259**, and the piano takes over the lead on the last quarter-note of **bar 263**.

The execution of the dynamic in **bars 283–304** is very difficult indeed. First a *p*, followed in the next bar by a *pp* which must not be as quiet as the final *decresc.* in **bar 301**, i.e., *quasi niente*. Here, for both partners, the instruction *kaum hörbar* ('scarcely audible'), which occurs in Webern, is appropriate. Different interpretations of the following *cresc.* have been offered: some interpreters are of the opinion that this *crescendo* should have a very quick development, and **bar 304** would then have to be a *p sub.*; others want to develop the *cresc.* from the *quasi niente* all the way to the *p*. I share the latter opinion, if only because the *p* on the last quarter-note of the violin in **bar 303** would otherwise make no sense.

Fingerings similar to those in **bars 235–248** of the violin seem requisite also in **bars 312–321**:

In the *p sub.* in **bar 323** the player should not forget that a *decresc.* leads to the *pp* in **bar 327**. The eighth-note figures in **bar 323** should be played short (best with jumpy bow) in the violin and *legato* in the piano, while in both parts the final quarter-note of every figure is shortened. The *cresc.* in **bar 329** and the *decresc.* in the following bar should reflect the agitation and be rich in dynamic contrast.

Sonata No. 5 in F major, Op. 24
(*Spring* Sonata)

Dedicated to Count Moritz von Fries
Manuscript preserved of the first three movements only;
fourth movement missing
Composed 1800–01,
together with the Piano Sonata, Op. 22,
and the Sonata for Piano and Violin, Op. 23
First edition October 1801, together with Op. 23

Introduction

This Sonata first appeared jointly with Op. 23 in October 1801. (The opus numbers were not divided until later.)

It is known as the *Spring* Sonata, not a title coined by the composer – as has happened to so many other pieces, in all musical genres. Incidentally, other similar nicknames for Beethoven's Violin Sonatas have come into use. In German-speaking countries, for example, the C minor Sonata, Op. 30, No. 2, is sometimes called the *Cockcrow* Sonata, obviously because of the almost 'unmotivated' *f* in the second movement in **bar 58** in the violin. The G major Sonata, Op. 30, No. 3, is often known as the *Champagne* Sonata (again, mainly in German-speaking countries). The *Kreutzer* Sonata, Op. 47, gets its name logically enough, however, for it was dedicated to the violinist Rodolphe Kreutzer, after Beethoven had cancelled the original dedication to George Bridgetower – rather as he did with Napoleon and the *Eroica*. Many of the titles later added by other (publishers') hands may describe the character of those works – especially for the less informed – rather well; and there is the further advantage that one knows instantly which work one is dealing with: the *Moonlight* or *Appassionata* Sonatas, *Pastoral* Symphony, *Rasumovsky* Quar-

Count Moritz von Fries
1777–1819

Important collector of art, music-lover and patron. He
was a partner in the Viennese banking house, Fries &
Co. As well as the A minor and F major Violin Sonatas,
Opp. 23 and 24, Beethoven dedicated to Fries the C
major String Quintet, Op. 29, and the Seventh Symphony, Op. 92. Haydn dedicated his last string quartet
to Fries, as did Schubert his song, *Gretchen am Spinnrade*.

tets, or, with Hadyn, the *Sunrise*, *Lark* or *Rider* Quartets; there
is Mozart's *Jupiter* Symphony, *Prussian* and *Dissonance* Quartets
(also known to German-speaking audiences as the *Karolinen-
Quartett*); and they occur even in Mendelssohn and Schumann
(the *Scottish*, *Italian* and *Rhenish* Symphonies, for example, all
had their titles added later) – hardly any of these titles
originated with the composer, although in our century composers have indeed given titles to some of their works (Strauss,
for example, in his *Symphonia Domestica* or Stravinsky with the
Symphony of Psalms).

Unfortunately the last movement of the autograph of the
Spring Sonata cannot be found, but we must count ourselves
lucky to possess the manuscript of at least most (the first three
movements) of this delightful work.

This Sonata, or parts of it, has been the province of many
amateur or other violinists who are not really advanced, with
the understandable result that in many places rather too
many slow tempi have come into use. (Once when I played
this Sonata in a BBC broadcast in London, some friends of
mine asked their ten-year old son, who was just learning the
work, how he had liked my performance. His answer was:
'Well, quite nice, but *much* too fast!') The second movement is
often dragged considerably and is frequently played in eighth-
notes instead of in quarter-notes. The scherzo loses in spirit
and wit if not performed rather fast, but the last movement
can stand a certain leisureliness, although the tempo designated is *alla breve*.

First Movement: *Allegro*

In the first movement I would advise the violinist to start with
an upbow, with which the natural phrasing gains dynamically
and tonally. It is amazing how few violinists can free themselves from that old bad habit which dictates the stereotyped
downbow on the stressed part of the bar and an upbow on
every upbeat. For instance, I begin the introduction in the
first movement of the Mozart A major Violin Concerto with
an upbow, but the upbeat of the main theme in the second

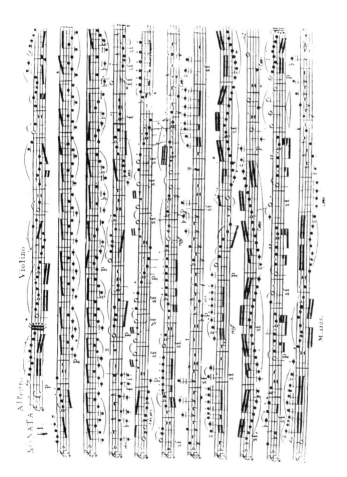

Sonata No. 5 in F major, Op. 24, *Spring*

Facsimile of first page of the violin part. The catalogue number at the bottom of the page reveals that although this is a later impression of the first edition it was issued nonetheless in Beethoven's lifetime.

movement with a downbow, which is still looked on as bizarre
although it should be clear to everyone that the *forte* with the
following *diminuendo* in the second and third bars is in keeping
with the natural pressure and the weight ratio of the bow:

60

Thus, too, one need only compare the dynamic in the first
theme of the *Spring* Sonata with that in **bars 134–141** in the
recapitulation, where even some *sfz*s are designated. All the
same, one should by no means adjust the dynamic in the first
occurrence of this material to that noted in the recapitulation.
The descending phrasing in **bars 4** and **6** comes very much
more naturally in the downbow. Many editions adapt **bar 7** to
the third and fifth bars, which was obviously not intended.
Bar 7, then, has divided bowing. The pianist should exercise
some restraint in the theme in **bars 11–17** and, in the
recapitulation, in **bars 124–132**, and resist the all-too-
common *cresc.* and *dim.*; it is far less pretentious, and much
more impressive, to perform this section without too much
romanticizing grandiloquence. The accompanying figure of
the violin in **bars 20–23** contains a charming bass line many
violinists overlook:

61

The same applies to **bars 144–147**.

An observation I consider very important: if one compares
**bars 28, 40–41, 44–45, 54–61, 90–97, 100–101, 104–
105, 108–109, 152, 164–165, 168–169** and **178–185** it
becomes clear that in this first movement most of the descending figures are written in quarter-notes while the ascending
ones are in eighth-notes. This means that one must clearly
differentiate, despite the dots, between the note-values of
quarter-notes and those of eighth-notes, i.e., the quarter-notes
must always be longer than the eighth-notes. Most interpreters overlook this notation and simply play everything

staccato – as short as possible. **Bars 37** and **161** have no more *sfz*s, and therefore, despite the *ff*, the two preceding *sfz*s must not be repeated (which, unfortunately, often happens). In **bars 38–49** the violinist should beware of interpreting the *sfz*s as *f*; they are all within a *p* phrase. This of course holds good also for the corresponding **bars 162–173**. In **bars 38–39, 42–43**, and the corresponding parallels, **bars 162– 163** and **166–167**, violinists very often play the *sfz* on the grace-notes, which is definitely wrong. The grace-notes should always be kept *p*, and the *sfz* on the main note *only*. The same observations apply to pianists (**bars 48, 50, 54–65, 90–97**, and **172, 174, 178–189**), who, in such cases, however, are often more conscientious than string players.

There are some older editions which in **bar 46** print an unjustified *f* for the violinist. Although the violin is leading in **bars 46–54** and **170–178**, with the exception of the *sfz* the whole phrase is *p*. Here the piano has an imitative role, but starting with **bars 62–70**, as with as **186–194**, it is the other way around: the piano leads, and the violin takes over as the imitator.

The *rinforzandi* printed in **bars 51, 67, 175** and **191** are often misundertood; we have here not merely an *sfz* on one note, but the *whole* bar is to be performed with extreme intensity and sustained strength of tone. In **bars 77** and **201** the first note in the violin part – in contrast to the two preceding bars – must be a continuation through the bar-line of the previous bar: no rest after the first quarter-note.

In **bars 89, 213**, and **215** a *non-legato* is printed for both instruments, i.e., notes only lightly separated but not too short. The transition to the recapitulation in **bars 121–123** presents some players with difficulties in ensemble, and thus the visual aid of an inaudible bow change by the violinists on every bar can be useful for the pianist. It is indeed embarrassing when the violinist arrives at his A while the pianist is playing G sharp!

In **bar 133** the violinist should conclude the preceding accompanying phrase with the first sixteenth-note A. The scale, which has the character of an upbeat, does not start until the second sixteenth-note; thus a tiny lengthening of the first note makes sense. A good many violinists end this run with a *diminuendo*, which is obviously not in accordance with the meaning, nor with the composer's intention. **Bar 134** is therefore a genuine *piano subito*.

In the main theme of the violin, in **bars 134–139**, the *sfz*s which are not noted at the beginning of the Sonata are given, but not the *cresc.*s which lead to the *sfz*s – as is clearly evident from the piano part in **bars 137** and **139**. To insert them is no sacrilege. The violinist should resist the habit of playing a *sfz* also in **bar 141**; this spot thereby acquires a special charm.

I have already pointed out in dealing with the exposition almost all the difficulties which occur in the recapitulation. From the beginning of the coda, starting with **bar 210**, the attention of the players should once more be drawn to the *non-legati* of **bars 213** and **215**. Nor should one neglect the *cresc.* in both instruments in the second half of **bar 214**, with the *p sub.* immediately following. The *cresc.* which begins in **bar 216** should, in my opinion, not be interrupted by the two *sfz*s; it leads up to the *p sub.* in **bar 222**. But there may be a difference of opinion here. In **bar 222** the piano shapes the essential main voice for two bars, together with the first eighth-note of the next bar, and I advise the violinist to take the lead only from the second eighth-note of **bar 224**. The intended *piano subito* in **bar 228**, after the *cresc.*, must not yet be understood as a *pp*, since another *decresc.* leads to the printed *pp*.

From **bar 232** onwards the essentials occur between the left hand of the piano and the violin; the accompanying figures of the right hand must therefore be discreet. **Bars 232–235** should be delicate and *dolce* from both partners, so that the *cresc.* in **bar 236** and the following *sfz* do not lose their dramatic effect. The dynamics specified by Beethoven from **bar 237** to the end should be followed meticulously.

With some violinists the triplet accompaniment unfortunately sounds like this:

62

which is a distortion of the rhythm.

Second Movement: *Adagio molto espressivo*

It is important to consider here the correct placement of the comma missing from the tempo indication. Does it mean *Adagio molto, espressivo* or *Adagio, molto espressivo?* The interpretation does have a certain influence on the tempo of the movement. From the purely musical point of view, I find the second interpretation more convincing and I therefore prefer slow quarter-notes to a rhythm based on eighth-notes.

The thirty-second-notes in **bar 2** of the piano, and similarly in **bar 10** of the violin, are often played too quickly and unrhythmically. In **bar 4** of the piano and **bar 12** of the violin we are again confronted with the question: do we or don't we use grace-notes after the trill? I feel one can do nicely without the grace-note, especially because the ornamentation is indicated in this movement with some precision (e.g., **bars 6–8**, **14–16**, **32**, **34–35**, and **48**). In **bars 6–7** and **14–15** performers often 'sin' dynamically by using a *diminuendo* in the passage of sixty-fourths, thus losing the intended effect of the *p sub*.

Let me point to the varying dynamic markings in the piano: only an accent in **bar 18** but an *sfz* in **bar 19**; similarly two bars later, in the violin in **bar 20**, just an accent with an *sfz* in **bar 21**. The *sfz* should in both cases be more dramatic than the accent (i.e., the note with the >). The pianist often overlooks the phrasing of **bar 21**: the last four sixteenth-notes are to be played in two groups of two notes each, i.e., with a slight shortening of the second and fourth notes. This applies also to the violin in the last four sixteenth-notes of **bar 23**.

It is advisable for the violinist to wait quietly for the *arpeggio* of the piano in **bar 23** and to delay slightly the entry on the second eighth-note.

Bars 25–26 should be phrased in the violin exactly as in the piano, the *sfz* in this case to be treated like an *fp*, the dynamic significance of which becomes evident also in **bar 27** in the piano. The sustained note F in **bar 28** in the violin could well do with an intensification of the vibrato coinciding with the *cresc.* prescribed. The two sixteenth-notes of the violin in **bars 30–31** should not be too short, despite the dots, so as not to blur the singing character of a slow movement.

The main theme of the violin, from **bar 38** in the minor, could, to my taste, sound a little more veiled than when it first occurs, in **bar 10**. I therefore recommend here (**bar 38**) the D string for the theme, to create in this way a clear contrast with the serene mood of the beginning. Then in **bar 40** I do not object to omitting the grace-notes after the trill. A non-tempered intonation by the violinist – otherwise hardly practicable – seems quite possible in the ensemble playing with the piano in **bars 44–46**, i.e., rather low in the first two bars, and then a leading-note (C sharp) in **bar 46**, that is to say, high, with increasing intensity of the vibrato which calms down in the *p sub.* in **bar 48**. Each D of the violin in **bar 50** should be a degree louder and more intense than the preceding one.

In **bar 54** the first sixteenth-note should not be viewed as the beginning of a new phrase, for this B flat concludes the previous thematic passage. The distribution of the *cresc.* in both instruments from **bar 54** to the *p sub.* in **bar 58** is to be treated carefully, i.e., not to be developed too quickly or too slowly but definitely leading up to a kind of *f* at the end of **bar 57**.

The three *p sub.*s in **bars 66, 68,** and **70** are to be taken entirely seriously. I would advise the violinist to look on the first quarter-note in **bar 70** as the close of the preceding phrase, so that the coda-like section actually begins with the second quarter-note. The thirty-second notes, **bars 70–72**, should in both instruments be played with extreme calm; a tiny *calando* in the penultimate bar seems natural.

Third Movement: *Scherzo. Allegro molto*

This movement has a jocular, earthy sense of humour; an unsophisticated audience thinks it merely unrhythmical ensemble. Canons can sometimes give rise to the same impression, although in such cases it is more obvious than in this movement. In the second part, in **bar 18**, the violinist must beware of playing a *cresc.* or even an *f*. In this bar in the *p* a jumping bow stroke can be used, whereas in **bar 20** in the *cresc. detaché* is best. The quarter-notes in **bars 26–27** must be clearly held longer by both instruments than the preceding eighth-notes, a point much too often neglected. Whether one goes into the trio without slowing the tempo or interpolates a short cæsura is a question of taste. I personally make a cæsura of about the length of a whole bar between scherzo and trio. The trio could be started *sautillé* by the violinist and in the *cresc.* more and more *à la corde*, which applies also to **bars 40–42**. The *da capo* I enter directly, with no break.

Fourth Movement: *Rondo. Allegro ma non troppo*

The manuscript of this movement, unfortunately, is missing, as I have mentioned. Although designated *alla breve*, the tempo indication does include a *ma non troppo*; and I therefore advise a leisurely tempo, which need by no means interfere with the intrinsically graceful character.

In the rondo theme the phrasing groups in the first, third and seventh bars are not sufficiently brought out, especially by pianists. Actually, it should sound (to exaggerate somewhat) like this:

63

Violinists run less danger of incorrect phrasing here, provided the bow stroke is executed as Beethoven indicates. On the other hand, in **bars 15** and **17** the *sfz*s are often undervalued by violinists and played rather colourlessly. In order to shorten the quarter-note before the trill with the grace-note in **bars 20–21** and **143–144** in the violin, I would recommend for these quarter-notes an upbow, and lifting as well. In the *sfz*s in the violin part in **bars 28–29** and **151–152**, there is often a tendency to provide the preceding sixteenth-note also with an accent, which is not desirable.

One should bear in mind the distribution between the two instruments of the upper and lower voices in **bars 38–49**, and similarly in **bars 161–182**. The violin leads from the third quarter-note of **bar 38** to the third quarter-note of **bar 40** and here the piano takes the lead. From the second half of **bar 42** the upper voice again belongs to the violin and passes to the piano again from the third quarter-note of **bar 44**. Although not so specified, the eighth-note figures in the left hand of the piano (**bars 40–47**) should be played short (compare the dots in similar places in **bars 167–180**). I would recommend that both instrumentalists treat with loving care the essential *cresc.* with the following *p sub.* in **bars 54–56** and **187–189**.

The insertions in the violin part in **bars 57** and **59** are in no way to be understood as sharply accentuated *sfz*s; they are merely a strengthening of the piano voice by adding an octave, which requires soft emphasis intensified by vibrato. The precisely noted dynamic of the secondary theme in **bars 73–105** is fascinating and entirely convincing but unfortunately it is frequently ignored. In **bar 99** the instruction *rinf.* is missing in the violin part, but in the piano part it is clearly indicated at this point as well as in the preceding corresponding **bar 91**. Here the deficiency must certainly be made up. Moreover, after the *rinf.* in both cases one should return to the *p* with a slight *dim.* so as not to anticipate the subsequent *cresc.*

The question of the dynamic in the accompaniment figure of this *rinf.* cannot be answered unequivocally. In **bar 91** the violin stays in *p*, but in **bar 99** it is not clear whether the pianist should execute the *rinf.* in both hands. I am inclined to leave the accompanying figure of the right hand in *p* and thereby to create a similar situation to that in **bar 91**.

What induced Beethoven to shape the phrasings of the almost identically repeated accompanying figure (**bars 73–104**) quite differently in the two parts I am at a loss to understand. Probably there are errors here, as the manuscript of this last movement is missing and one cannot always rely on first editions. I would also point out the following discrepancies: the second half of **bar 85** is printed an octave higher in the right hand of the piano part than in the violin part in **bar 77**, which is still acceptable as a variant; but it is incomprehensible why **bar 80** of the violin and **bar 88** of the piano do not agree.

Bar 80, violin part:

64

Bar 88, piano part:

65

The *accelerando* written rhythmicly into the piano part in **bars 109–111** gives many violinists a bit of a headache, for where there are obscurities of a rhythmic kind or the wrong use of pedalling, the violin entry (**bar 112**) is put at unnecessary risk. The pianist's strict observance of the printed rhythmic subdivision not only corresponds to the actual text, quite apart from the exact following of the dynamic (two bars *cresc.* with a *p sub.* in **bar 112**), but will also guarantee an impeccable ensemble here.

The phrasing in the violin part in **bars 117–121** is badly neglected most of the time. Without knowledge of the piano's thematic material, most violinists phrase the entries in these bars in two-bar groups. However, if one looks at the piano part, things are quite different:

66

As can be seen, the violin part should adapt itself to the upbeat phrasing of the piano theme.

As usual, the violinist is more visible than audible in the *pizz.* passages in **bars 124–131** and **193–196**. All *pizzicati* are usually produced too softly, and it is often grotesque to watch how the string players try to make clear their musical intentions by mime, but without a sound emerging.

On the second note of **bar 206** in the violin, as also in the
piano part, a *forte* is missing, for in **bar 212** on the third
quarter-note a *p* appears, which should be observed by the
violinist, too, on the sixth eighth-note.

We find the same in **bars 215–221**; the piano part *f* from
the second note of **bar 215** and the violin *f* in this same bar.
From the second half of **bar 221**, both instruments *p*.

In the coda from **bar 224**, let me refer both players to the
written dynamic. For **bar 227** in the piano and **bars 231** and
235 in the violin I recommend grace-notes after the trill, but
not for **bar 234**. From **bar 236** to the end the phrasing of
staccato notes and slurs should be clearly brought out, but in
the dynamics one should so proceed that the last two bars still
get a clear intensification, i.e., an *ff* compared to the previous *f*.

Sonata No. 6 in A major, Op. 30, No. 1

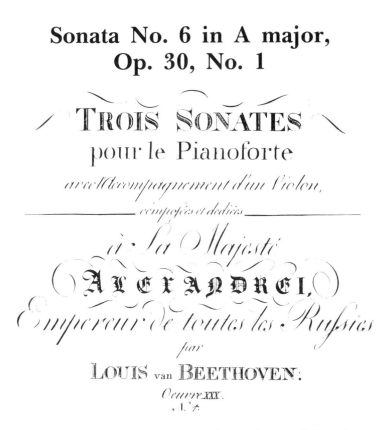

Dedicated to the Emperor Alexander I of Russia
Manuscript: Öffentliche Wissenschaftliche Bibliothek, East Berlin
Composed 1802
First edition 1803

Introduction

The Sixth Sonata, in A major (incidentally, three of the Violin Sonatas are in A major), is a work for which I have a very special affection. Unfortunately it can also be heard but

rarely. Possibly my affection is based, among other things, on
the fact that this Violin Sonata does not enjoy general
popularity, and I regard its neglect as a real wrong – rather as
a child little valued by its family and treated with neglect often
receives sympathy for this very reason. I feel the first two
movements to be especially serious, profound and masterly.

The second movement, the *Adagio molto espressivo*, belongs
for me among the most beautiful and moving things that have
ever been expressed in music.

The last movement – although also magnificent – does not,
in my view, quite reach the level of achievement of the other
two. Originally the last movement was meant for the *Kreutzer*
Sonata, Op. 47, but quite rightly was later exchanged by
Beethoven. Not only is the present third movement of the
Kreutzer Sonata more suitable for the whole work, but an
additional variation movement like the one in Op. 30, No. 1
would be inappropriate after the second movement of the
Kreutzer Sonata, which is also a variation movement. The
exchange could be made all the more easily as both movements are in A major.

First Movement: *Allegro*

It is really hardly necessary to mention that the piano has the
lead in the first eight bars. I do so all the same because
violinists tend to give too much importance to their *obbligato*
function. Here the violinist must content himself with playing
'second fiddle'; anyway, he comes into his own later as he
plays the upper voice in **bars 10–19**. In **bars 17** and **166** to
my mind a grace-note should follow the trill in both instruments. In the whole Sonata, but especially in the first
movement, almost all the trills should be provided with
grace-notes. Beethoven occasionally wrote out these ornaments himself, but they are not consistently printed. The
sharp dynamic contrasts which Beethoven often provided
with an almost excessive exactitude play an essential role in
this work too.

One should take care not to use *diminuendi* to lead to the *p*, or

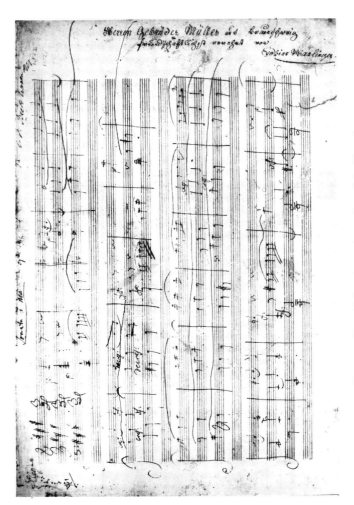

Sonata No. 6 in A major, Op. 30, No. 1

The notorious illegibility of Beethoven's manuscripts was largely a feature of his later life. This first page of the Sixth Sonata reveals that, in 1802 at least, he was still capable of a script that did not give his copyists too much trouble.

crescendi to the *f* as the case may be, where they are not expressly asked for. The *sfzs* in the piano in **bars 28–31** and **177–179** are to be sharply accentuated in spite of the whole phrase being in *f*; too often there is hardly any difference from the other quarter-notes to be heard. The dynamic notation in the violin part in **bars 31** and **180** is utopian, for in the piano there is still an *sfz* and the original *f* continues undiminished. In this case, the violin should not play *p* but continue a strong *mf*; otherwise it is inaudible. Finally, the violin part here represents a complement to the left hand of the piano, and is to be dynamically balanced accordingly. Another interpretation could be that the left hand here could already achieve a *dim.* while the violin could proceed exactly the same, i.e., either

The dots printed above or below the quarter-notes are of interest, and must be adhered to strictly by the pianist but only up to and including the first note in **bar 31** (and **180**). The following chords of the left hand (on the second and third quarter-notes in **bars 31** and **180** respectively) should sound softer and longer, which is also indicated by the *legato* notation of the violin. The precisely indicated last quarter-note of **bars 33** and **186** is, for me, a source of particular delight; to my sorrow all too many pianists play inexactly here, and so: really short in the right hand, long in the left, and softly slurred to the next bar. In the development this inspiration of genius is varied, in that in **bar 94** the friction of G sharp and G natural assumes the same function. As mentioned already, gracenotes after the trills, in **bars 35–36** in the piano and **43–44** in the violin, are imperative, for in **bars 96–97**, **188**, and **196**

they are specified by Beethoven himself. Here we have again a classic example of how senseless the blind following of an Urtext can be. As a violinist I would not baulk at playing in **bars 48** and **201** a *cresc.* adapted to the piano part, although not expressly so noted. It seems illogical that the accompanying figure in the piano should overpower the leading voice in the violin. We now come to an interesting change in Beethoven's dynamic in a passage that is virtually identical: in **bars 60** and **64** in the exposition, as in **bars 213** and **217** in the recapitulation, one should observe the *decresc.* which is missing in the development, in **bars 131** and **135**. I consider this change deliberate.

In **bar 69**, and also **222**, the build-up of the three-voice chord should be presented with clarity:

I would accentuate lightly each new voice in spite of the *pp*. The same idea can be found in **bars 142–148**.

The figure

in **bars 70–72** and **76–78**, like the figure

in **bars 223–225** and **229–231** appears each time in a three-fold repetition. It would be rather unimaginative to execute this figure three times in exactly the same way, and I propose for the third time, as a final version or summing-up, as it were, a slight calming down or stretching which, in this case, takes us further. The slurring written for the violin part in **bars 79** and **232** seems to me more logical and more persuasive than the phrasing at the same place in the piano part in **bars 73** and **226**:

Incidentally, one should compare **bars 79−81** with **bars 232−234** in the violin part. The dynamic should be adapted, of course, in the first case to the corresponding bars of the recapitulation, i.e., a *p* also in the violin part on the first quarter-note of **bar 228**. In **bar 102** a *p* in the piano part seems to be missing. The two separate *cresc.*s in **bars 101** and **104** would not make much sense if the phrase did not begin in *p*, as in **bar 106**. Both instrumentalists should strictly observe the difference between *p* and *pp* in **bars 136** and **138**. In the coda the *sfz*s in the piano in **bar 236**, and in the violin in **bar 240**, do not interrupt the prevailing *p*. In **bars 242−246** both instruments must aim at complete accord in the dynamic development, while in the last two bars the violin brings the movement to a consummate end with the figure fundamental to the whole *allegro*.

Second Movement: *Adagio molto espressivo*

To my mind this *Adagio* ranks among the most beautiful and most important pieces ever written for violin and piano. It is a deeply serious and moving confession, the end of which equals the late Beethoven in its rapture. A perfect interpretation can be attained only with difficulty, for it presupposes real inner maturity and calm, even contemplative detachment, on the part of the players which they too often underestimate. Rhythmicly, there are delicate problems to be overcome here, as, for instance, the absolute precision of the thirty-second notes in theme and accompaniment.

    The last two eighth-notes in the theme of **bars 2** and **4**, as also **10** and **12**, are provided with dots, but also with a slur. For pianists this is an indication of a *non-legato*; the violinist should understand what this means and play these notes slightly detached but long. With the upbeat in **bar 8** the piano already takes the lead, and here I recommend to the violinist a fingering which elucidates the structure and dynamic of what is going on:

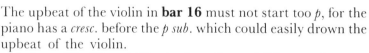

74

The upbeat of the violin in **bar 16** must not start too *p*, for the piano has a *cresc*. before the *p sub*. which could easily drown the upbeat of the violin.

In **bars 23–25** and **50**, pianists often exhibit a tendency to rush, even to play unrhythmically. Could it be that the many thirty-second and sixty-fourth-note cross-bars have a hypnotic influence?

The piano's *fermata* in **bar 26** should not be extended unduly; beside the question of musical proportion, this has a practical reason as well, for the violinist must neither shorten his long F sharp nor split the bowing.

In the piano part the instructions for a *p* on the first quarter-notes of **bars 44–46** and **48–49** are missing; they must of course be supplied.

In **bar 47** I would recommend a soft *martelé* to the violinist, a way of bowing which is out of fashion these days and, regrettably, is used far too rarely. The usual substitution of *spiccato* does not have the same quality, but is somewhat easier of execution. One can assist, convincingly, the dramatic heightening in **bars 52–53** of the violin – which demands a steep *cresc*. within a short space of time – by a gradual intensification of the vibrato, i.e., starting with almost no vibrato in **bar 52**.

Beethoven, unfortunately, was not as exact as Mozart in his instructions on the length of grace-notes. Mozart almost always specified the intended length of grace-notes very precisely as $\mathquad\text{♩} = ♪ = ♪$ and even $♪$. In the present instance I would interpret the grace-notes in the piano in **bars 57** and **59** strictly as short. The inexactitude of these time-values can be gauged, for instance, from the fact that in early editions, and also in the first edition, the grace-note in **bar 58** is written as a sixteenth-note, whereas in the manuscript and in later editions it is given as a thirty-second!

Bar 63 frequently gives rise to differences of opinion between the players, and thus the result in the ensemble playing can occasionally turn out rather unhappily. My proposal is:

75

The second half of **bar 69** is rather complicated, as the left and right hands in the piano – as in the violin part – have been laid out in different rhythms. Many interpreters consider the strict observance of these notations to be splitting hairs; personally, I find it attractive to keep fully to the rhythmic lay-out and not to create baroque-style adaptations.

The ineffable tenderness which begins in **bar 79** and is repeated in **bar 91** requires self-denial of the kind so often called for in ancient Chinese proverbs. After one of my concerts the great pianist Artur Schnabel paid me an exceptional compliment: 'I thank you not only for what you have done but even more for what you abstained from'.

In **bar 90** I would propose that the pianist execute the mordent as follows:

76

In **bar 94**, too, there must be a clear rhythmic division between violin and piano.

For many violinists the ties from the last eighth-note of **bars 97–98** to the following bars present problems: players often

incorrectly make a separation between the two A's. The
notation would not be so easily misunderstood if the dot (as in
my version) were placed outside the slur. Thus the dot under
the second eighth-note A is to be regarded here only as a
shortening of the note-value:

Whether the pianist holds down the pedal in the last
one-and-a-half bars or interrupts in accordance with the
eighth-note rest in the left hand remains a matter of taste.

Third Movement: *Allegretto con Variazioni*

As I mentioned in my introduction to this Sonata, this
movement was originally the last movement of the *Kreutzer*
Sonata, Op. 47. The decision to exchange these two last
movements was wise, for not only does the new arrangement
better suit the character of the music, but two variation
movements following one upon the other (as would have
happened in the original version) must remain of somewhat
doubtful effectiveness.

Despite Beethoven's masterly control of variation technique
(one need only think of the many downright banal themes he
developed in an unbelievable, even fantastic way), this movement cannot be counted one of his best – which is particulrly
regrettable if only because it follows directly upon the soaring
heights of the preceding movement. This slight falling-away in
quality in last movements is something that occurs in many
composers (occasionally, for example, in Brahms), and it is
always our good fortune when it does not occur. For me, at
any event, the variations of this movement are much more
important than their pleasant but hardly brilliant theme.

In the first part of the theme, after each four bars, a
noticeable change in character can be found. **Bars 1–4** and
9–12 are lyrical and graceful, but the following ones resemble
a rural and rather robust dance. And the last variation is of a
similar split character.

To me it seems hardly desirable to add to the three *sfz*s in **bars 6–7** and **14–15** yet a fourth *sfz* in the next bar, although this happens all too often.

The grace-notes in the second part of the theme are printed with rhythmic differences in various editions. In **bars 19** and **27** in the Henle edition, as in the manuscript, the first grace-note is written as an eighth-note but the second as a sixteenth-note. In the older Joachim edition all the grace-notes discussed here are short. In the first edition the first grace-note in the violin part in **bar 19** is also an eighth-note and the second a sixteenth-note as in Henle; in contrast, in the piano part in **bar 27** in the first edition both grace-notes are printed as sixteenth-notes. I do not believe we should take the significance of these divergences too seriously. Musically, and instinctively, I tend to play both grace-notes short in the violin part, as in the piano.

A further problem is that of the added ornamentation in **bar 30** in the piano, which is missing in the parallel place in the violin part in **bar 22**. Here I assume the intention of the composer was to shape this bar differently. In **bar 30** the grace-note in the piano part is clearly notated as D sharp; hence the natural on the D later in the bar. All this is missing in the violin part in **bar 22**. Nevertheless, it is quite conceivable to adapt the violin part.

I should say something here about the closing of the theme: at the end of each of Variations I, II, IV and V a *p* is written. As a *forte* ending to the theme does not convince me, I return to the *p* after the *sfz* in **bars 22** and **30**, although it is not specifically indicated.

Variation I

The violinist has some difficulties to overcome here. First, let us note that the character of this variation is virtuosic, elegant and graceful. The pianist plays short *staccato* notes throughout, so that if the violinist were to use a long *détaché* the effect would be rather clumsy. All notes with dots should therefore be played *sautillé* with the exception of those which are written above or below the last note of a slur. In my notation it would look like this:

Bar 36: 78

Bar 41: 79

Many pianists play the last bass note on the third quarter of the final bar because they haven't looked at the text closely enough; this is understandable in view of the last bars of Variations II, III and IV but it is simply incorrect in Variation I.

Variation II

In the second part the *legato* notes of the left hand of the piano should serve not only as accompanying bass notes but as an expressive counterpart rather like a cello. In the *prima volta* of the second part the last three notes of the violin (although not specifically noted as in the first part) should also be phrased as an upbeat, i.e., here too one can divide the bow as before:

80

Variation III

Unfortunately, dynamic markings are missing here, with the exception of the *sfz*s throughout the variation, the *cresc.* in **bar 69** and the *p* in **bar 75**.

The character of this variation I find rather energetic, already conditioned by its position between two more delicate variations. Here, of course, opinions may differ. Something like the following dynamic would be according to my ideas (which, in any case, are subjective and intended only to clarify): in **bar 65** both voices *f*; for **bar 68** both *dim.*; then the specified *cresc.* should be carried on to the *sfz*. The upbeat in **bar 72** continues with a *cresc.* to the *f*; the *p sub.* in **bar 75** applies to the violin also. In the next bar, again for both instruments, there should be a *cresc.* to the *f*, which in the piano starts on the fourth quarter-note of **bar 76** but in the violin not until the second quarter-note of **bar 77**. In the *prima volta* of the second part, also for both instruments, there should be a *cresc.* on the upbeat. There remains the question of the trills: with or without grace-notes? My plea would be for grace-notes in **bar 67** for the piano, and in **bar 71** for both instruments, and in **75** and **79** for the piano again, the last time perhaps with a slight difference:

81

Variation IV

The *p*s written in the chords for the violin pose certain problems for the player: either they sound too loud, that is, not really *p*, or are spread so much that they are at rhythmic variance with the piano chords. I play these *p* chords as very quick *arpeggii* at the tip of the bow – not first two strings and then the other two; always only one string at a time but quickly, to obtain as far as possible the impression of the simultaneous sounding of all the notes of the chord; and in the *cresc.* I use correspondingly more bow.

Bar 86 is given incorrectly in many editions, for in the manuscript and in the first edition a *p* is expressly demanded immediately after the *ff*; that is, *ffp* and not *ff* ($>$) with a *p* in the next bar. **Bar 95** is also open to doubt, as in almost all editions, and in the manuscript, the *p* is noted at the beginning of the bar but in the first edition not until the second quarter-note. Both versions are possible.

Variation V

The enchanting violin counterpoint in this variation seduces many interpreters into regarding the theme itself in the piano (this time in the minor, with occasional *fugato* inserts) as subordinate. I consider theme and counter-melody to be of equal value here, so that there should be no division into one leading and one *obbligato* voice. As for the rhythmic values of the grace-notes in **bars 115** and **123**, I would adapt them to the realization in the theme.

Although everyone should draw his own conclusions from this, I feel I have to point out these contradictions and with them to offer my own conceptions. The different dynamics of **bars 103–105** compared with **bars 111–113** are significant and should not be adjusted at all. For the information of the pianist, I should like to point out the difference in the notation of **bars 129–130** in the first printing and later editions. In the later editions we find:

and in the first edition:

which means practically the same.

The manuscript corresponds to the first edition with the exception of **bar 129**; there the chord of the left hand is written as a whole note, not the half-note of the first edition.

All dots above or below the eighth-notes in **bars 130–151** are again to be understood as shortenings and in my notation would be outside the slur:

84

In **bar 138** the *appoggiatura* of the violin – in contrast to the preceding rhythm – is to be played before the bar line, and the first quarter-note of the piano comes only on the main note (D) of the violin.

Variation VI: *Allegro, ma non tanto*

As I mentioned when discussing the theme, here too the change in character after the first four bars is evident; thus one should begin with the *dolce* and, from the fifth bar, start the *cresc.* plus the printed *staccato* notes.

The trills in **bars 154, 158, 162** and **166** I would play as a mordent:

85

86

It is interesting that the second note of the fourth bar of the theme is written in the piano part as an eighth-note and in the violin as a quarter-note. But this quarter-note of the violin has a dot outside the slur so that it can be equated to the eighth-note of the piano.

In the second half of **bars 159** and **167** a *decresc.* seems to be missing in the piano, for the following accompaniment should be played quietly in accordance with the *dolce*; thus the *cresc.* in **bar 164** can be justified. There are but few pianists who follow Beethoven's phrasing in **bars 168, 172** and **174** and realize them as genuine groups of two.

The short eighth-notes of the violin in **bars 168–170** and **172–173** are better played as *martelé*, in order to create a contrast in both character and sound with the next bar, which is more attractive as *spiccato*.

Bars 177–179 in the violin part have a much more elegant effect if they are delivered in *sautillé*. Just as the piano in **bars 168**, **172** and **174** phrases the sixteenth-notes in groups of two, so should the violin in **bar 182**. The inspired coda strikes one as almost uncanny; it too shows the 'split' character I have already discussed. The mood which in the beginning is no longer earth-bound and is inward-looking changes considerably from the *cresc.* in **bars 194** and **216**. The repeated knocking effect of the notes in both instruments in **bars 190–193**, **206–209** and **212–215** can be provided with tiny accents, despite the *pp*, to give an appropriate degree of expression to the distant tolling of the death-knell. The violin trill in **bars 197** and **219** is again played as a mordent, as in **bars 158** and **166**:

87

Although in the first edition the last three eighth-notes of **bars 197** and **219** are tied, in the manuscript there is a visible indication that only the first eighth-notes are to be tied; the last eighth-note is separate and short. In the manuscript it looks like this:

88

Each *p sub.* from **bar 220** to **232** is an essential component of the expression and should not be weakened or diluted. The optimistic final bars (from **bar 220**) bring this Sonata, with its rich contrasts of solemnity and mourning with gaiety and affirmation, to a radiant close.

Sonata No. 7 in C minor, Op. 30, No. 2

Dedicated to Emperor Alexander I of Russia
Manuscript: Collection of H.C. Bodmer, Zurich
Composed 1802
First Edition 1803

Introduction

The C minor Sonata, Op. 30, No. 2, is one of Beethoven's most popular Violin Sonatas and, along with the *Spring* and *Kreutzer* Sonatas, is played much more often than all the others. Its superlative qualities make this work one of the most impressive compositions of its kind, and Joseph Szigeti rightly speaks[1] of 'its epic drama, cast in such a heroic mould (so difficult to do justice to)' – although it would be regrettable to neglect other Beethoven Sonatas on account of this one. The tension of expression in the outer movements and the consistency of their headlong pace – as in the A minor Sonata, Op. 23, and the *Kreutzer* Sonata, Op. 47 – are among the richest and most admirable qualities of this Sonata; it is a tremendously spirited, gripping piece, full of passion and powerful strength.

Although the second (slow) movement offers a soothing contrast to the first and fourth, it is often delivered in too slow a tempo, whereby the listener sometimes loses the thread. It must be remembered, moreover, that long notes on a keyboard instrument (other than an organ) do not have the same sustaining power as in a stringed instrument and therefore that the piano cannot achieve the same effect in the repetition of the thematic material. The choice of tempo

[1] *op. cit.*, p. 31.

Alexander I, Emperor of Russia
23 December 1777–1 December 1825

The dedication of the three Sonatas, Op. 30, to Czar Alexander I initially went unacknowledged and without financial reward. It was not until early 1815 that this omission was rectified:

In a conversation with Beethoven one day, Bertolini [Dr Andreas Bertolini, Beethoven's friend and his doctor from 1806 to 1816] suggested to him that, as polonaises were then so much in vogue, he should compose one and dedicate it to the Empress of Russia [then in Vienna for the Congress]; for, perhaps, thereby he might also obtain some acknowledgement from Emperor Alexander for the dedication to him of the Violin Sonatas, Op. 30 – for none had ever been made. . . . Beethoven was admitted to an audience with the Empress and presented the polonaise [Op. 89], for which he received a present of 50 ducats. On this occasion he was asked if he had ever received anything from the Czar? As he had not, a hundred ducats was added for the Sonatas.

Thayer, *op. cit.*, p. 603

should, I feel, be guided by the thirty-second-note figuration in the piano part of the recapitulation from **bar 60**.

The scherzo, too, is in a more cheerful mood; the effect of the agitation of the last movement is thus all the more dramatic. The tempo of the last movement should not be 'as fast as possible', for the coda still requires a considerable intensification.

First Movement: *Allegro con brio*

The dot indicated in each case in **bars 2**, **4**, **10** and **12** should again be understood as a shortening and in my orthography would be placed outside the slur. As I have already stressed at various points above (especially with regard to the *Spring* Sonata, Op. 24), players should in general pay more attention to the difference between dots with or without slurs, above all when they originate from a composer who was principally a pianist. With slurs a dot means *non-legato* and should definitely be played with longer note values than where a pure *staccato* is indicated. Thus the quarter-notes in **bar 6** are often played much too short; this happens also in **bars 130** and **137**. The left hand of the piano in **bars 10**, **12**, **46–51**, **140**, **142** and **179–184** is often too loud or too indistinct, and occasionally even both!

The two consecutive *cresc*.s in **bars 17–18** of the violin sometimes give rise to perplexity. In fact, the two *cresc*.s are intentional, for **bars 147–148** are also marked in this way, where the two *sfz*s in the piano part make it clear.

I would advise both partners to use a small *dim*. at the end of **bar 17**, but in the succeeding bar a *cresc*. to the following *sfz*. Unfortunately most pianists follow the dynamic in **bar 26** inexactly; the second quarter-note should be the note which is slightly reinforced. The secondary theme in **bar 29** plus upbeat brings technical bowing problems, for unplanned bow division can easily cause wrong and unintended accents. As a possible solution the following could be considered:

In **bars 38** and **171** of the piano part the marking *sempre staccato* is missing in the first edition and in the manuscript but it does occur in both cases in the violin part and applies to the piano as well. Likewise, in the first edition and in the manuscript, in **bar 32** the *sfz* of the violin and in **bar 42** that of the left hand of the piano are missing, but in the recapitulation in **bars 165** and **175** they are present.

The scales in the violin in **bars 47**, **49**, **52**, **54**, **180** and the first half of **bar 182** can be played satisfactorily in *sautillé*. Both partners should be careful not to reach an *f* too early, i.e., before **bar 51**, and respectively **bar 184**, and also holds true for the *cresc.* before the *f* in **bars 57** and **190**.

All the last slurred notes in **bars 52–57** as well as **185–190** in the piano part, and in the violin in **bars 63–67** and **196–200**, should be shortened, as mentioned before in parallel passages:

The trills in **bars 61** and **194** of the piano should in my opinion be played with grace-notes.

In **bars 62** and **195** we encounter another of those contradictory dynamic markings: in the piano part the *p* is printed both times at the beginning of the bar, but in the violin we find the *p* – this is consistent with the manuscript and first edition – on the second eighth-note the first time, but at the beginning of the bar in the recapitulation. I am inclined to play the *p* in the violin too at the beginning of the bar both times.

The dynamic of **bars 75** and **77** given for the piano

should also be employed in **bars 79, 81, 83, 85, 87, 89** and **91** and in the recapitulation in **bars 208–214**. The *p sub.* in **bars 82** and **88** in the piano part is written in different places, in the first case at the beginning of the bar, in the second not until the second quarter-note. Because of the notation for the violin and for obvious musical reasons I believe that in **bar 82** (as the second time) the *p* should not be realized until the second quarter-note.

In order to mould the three-bar *cresc.* really dramatically it is absolutely necessary to start **bar 92** in both instruments as quietly as possible. And the last three eighth-notes of **bars 98** and **100** should be played with an almost exaggerated *crescendo*.

The note-values in the left hand of the piano (**bars 107–112**) are given differently, i.e., in eighth-notes, with the exception of **bar 108** where they are in sixteenth-notes. The eighth-notes, however, have dots which are missing on the sixteenth-notes. It is clear that in spite of the difference in notation the same note-length is intended – further proof of how complicated it is even for a composer to interpret his own conceptions in such a way that others, too, can understand them!

I would play **bar 112** in the violin *martelé* as here this is more in character with the *marcato* of the piano than it would be in *spiccato*. A style of bowing like *martelé* cannot be replaced by jumpy bowings, and I regret very much that the majority of violinists today neglect the *martelé*.

Many violinists have difficulty in making a really precise entry in **bars 114** and **118**. The reason for this can be that the violinist hears the ascending chromatic line as if the strong beat of the bar were in this chromatic line. It is indeed more easily heard in this way:

92

But the violinist who studies it must have it clear in his mind that here the pedal G always falls on the strong beat:

On the other hand, a wrong or careless accentuation from the pianist can also be the cause of the difficulty.

In the first edition, apart from the correct *pp* in **bar 115**, there is also a *pp* in **bar 119**. The latter is certainly an error, for not only is a *p* written in the piano part in **bar 119** with a *decresc.* in the next bar but it also seems completely sensible that both instruments in **bar 115** play *pp* but in **bar 119** on the other hand only *p*, with the subsequent *decresc.* in **bar 120** which leads to the *pp* only in **bar 121**. (Incidentally, the dynamic is written correctly in the manuscript.) The syncopated octaves of the violin in **bars 123–124** should have accents which increase in strength each time.

In almost all editions a pedal sign is given from **bar 216** up to the third quarter-note in **bar 218** which is missing in the autograph as it is in the first edition. Beethoven's marking *senza sordino* in **bar 216** instead of the *ped.* noted above and *con sordino* in **bar 219** does mean the same thing, but I feel I should point this out to the reader.

Further dynamic notations in this movement which are paid insufficient attention are the *p* in **bar 221** and the *pp* in the next bar. There is a further problem in **bar 230**: does the *cresc.* lead to the *p*, or is it again a *p sub.*? I prefer, in accordance with Beethoven's style, the second option, but this is simply a question of personal taste.

The pianist should observe all the dynamic markings in the coda as precisely as possible. Pianists especially tend, because of certain technical difficulties, to play the *f* in **bar 247** as an *ff*, with the disadvantage of not being able to increase the volume further in **bar 252**.

Second Movement: *Adagio cantabile*

In my introduction to this Sonata I said that the tempo of this second movement should not be taken too slowly. The calm pace – neither hurried nor dragged – of the thirty-second-

notes of **bars 60–68** in the piano part is, for me, the guide to
the basic tempo of this *Adagio*. In accordance with the
character and also because of the *alla breve* signature one
should certainly avoid thinking in eighths!

The dynamic in the main theme is frequently misunderstood or treated carelessly: the *sfz* in **bar 3** does not arrest the
cresc. which is not cancelled until the *p sub.* in the next bar.
Thus it should be carried on, as should the violin in **bars
11–12**. In fact, in the manuscript and the first edition the *p* in
bar 12 of the violin part is missing, but it is clear that one
should proceed here exactly as in the piano part; so too in the
recapitulation where in **bar 64**, even in the violin part, the *p* is
clearly noted.

Mordents are frequently executed in rather a pedantic
manner, as, for instance, in **bars 7** and **59** in the piano and
bars 15 and **67** in the violin. Most of the time they are
arranged rhythmically like this:

94

whereby the rising line, i.e., the G, is anticipated – hence my
version

95

so that the grace-note too is played as a full sixteenth-note.
Many pianists tend to play the four sixteenth-notes on the
second quarter-note of **bar 16** as short *staccato* notes; but the
slur which is also there points to the fact that we are dealing
here with a *non-legato*, i.e., sung, as it were, lightly separated
long notes.

The dots on the second quarter-notes of **bars 17–18**,
25–26, **69–70**, and **77–78**, as I have already mentioned
before, shorten the note values.

The entry of the violin in **bar 22** should, as far as is possible,
go unnoticed and should strive for tonal and dynamic unity

with the piano, for up to the beginning of **bar 23** the violin plays the lower third here, so that the main line lies in the piano. In **bar 24**, as almost everywhere in Beethoven, the question arises of whether or not one should supply the trills with grace-notes. Here, as in **bars 31**, **75**, **84** and **92**, I would plead earnestly for a grace-note, in contrast to the last two quarter-notes in **bars 70** and **79**, on which in the next bar there follows a grace-note written by the composer himself – his intention is clear and unmistakable here. The notes supplied with dots in **bars 23** and **31** should be played not too short by either instrument, i.e., *non-legato*.

The true *staccato* notation of **bars 33–47** now appears in clear contrast to the *non-legato* which we found earlier. All the same, these *staccati* should not be played too short, for they are part of a slow, song-like movement, and must not give any impression of grotesquerie. Full-length thirty-second-notes with rests of the same length are what I have in mind here:

96

The following observation on rhythm should be considered especially carefully: in **bar 36** the last note of the violin comes only after the last sixteenth-note of the piano, and the pianist does well to stretch the last notes somewhat, if only because of the subsequent *p sub.* The same applies – with the roles reversed – to **bar 40**.

Although a *p* is not indicated until **bar 47**, I do not feel we should infer from this a continued *crescendo* from **bars 43** to **47**. I tend to favour a *dim.* in the violin in second half of **bars 45–46**, so that the beginning of **bar 46** also starts *p* in both instruments. There is, of course, room here for difference of opinion, but one should beware of confusing the *p* in **bar 47** with a *pp*, for in **bar 48** a *decresc.* will still be required which only then leads to the *pp*. Whether the *cresc.* in **bar 49** leads to a *p sub.* or only from the *pp* to the *p* is a matter of opinion – or a point of controversy. Personally, I believe in a *p sub.*, not only from knowledge of Beethoven's habits but because one *cresc.* following so soon after another would not have to be written twice unless an interruption were intended. The volume of the violin entry in **bar 51** must (despite being marked *p*) conform to the degree of loudness of the piano, whose *crescendo* has already begun.

The *staccato* notes in the violin part in **bars 54−60** again should not be too short, independently of the dynamic. The *f* of the violin in **bar 58** is a really bizarre idea, and many violinists shy away from complying fully with the dynamic demanded, but it was precisely this unexpected and extravagant idea that led to the popular German nickname of *Cockcrow* Sonata.

The grace-notes in **bar 68** of the piano are sometimes, wrongly, played too long, which makes the subsequent four thirty-second-notes become quintuplets.

In the triplet figure of **bars 85−87** and **93−95** there are four different indications of the length of the notes:

1. without dots or slurs;
2. *staccato* notation, i.e., dots;
3. slurs; and
4. dots with slurs, i.e., *non-legato*.

I find the distinction convincing in only three cases: *legato*, *non-legato* and *staccato*. The triplets without dots in my opinion are equivalent to the *non-legato*, i.e., not *staccato*.

The different note-lengths at the end of each C major scale in **bars 87−88** and **96−97** are not to be taken literally. It is not clear why the end-notes should sometimes be quarter-notes and other times eighth-notes. In **bar 96**, in a strict realization, the third quarter-note would continue to sound during the run of the right hand of the piano, and (when prescribed rests are observed) this would not be the case either before or afterwards. Such oversights creep in with a good many composers who are writing hurriedly, and they occur again and again with Beethoven – further proof of how unreasonable it is to accept an Urtext uncritically. In **bars 90−91** and **99−100**, the continuation of the melodic line is divided between the two instruments, which we find frequently in Beethoven – in the first case:

and in the second:

Accordingly the uniform application of a sustained *p* in the two instruments would not aid in clarifying the melodic line for the listener.

Pizzicati on the violin are not always as satisfying as those on lower string instruments, and so there is often here, in **bars 101–105**, insufficient resonance, and for several reasons: often a short, dry tonal quality results from a vibrato wrongly applied, which, after all, should promote lengthening. The string cannot reverberate when the finger pressure is interrupted by the vibrato. *Pizzicati*, furthermore, are usually executed too softly, giving rise to the absurd situation where the violinist, like a well-behaved child, is seen but not heard.

I would recommend that the pianist adapt as far as possible the eighth-notes of the right hand in **bars 105–106** to the preceding *pizz.* of the violin with regard to sound and also length of notes. In the continuation of **bars 107–110** in the bass, the eight-notes can gradually be lengthened. (In the manuscript and the first edition the piano part has the last two chords marked *senza sordino* and not, as in all later editions, *Ped.*[2])

---

[2] Even today it infuriates me when I think back on how an irresponsible and ignorant engineer ruined my Decca recording of this Sonata when transferring it from tape to disc by simply leaving off the last two chords of the slow movement because he assumed the movement was finished. It was incomprehensible, moreover, that Decca, for whom I had recorded all the Beethoven Sonatas, allowed the disc to reach the market in this condition. Fortunately many purchasers believed that they had here a recent discovery of a so-called Urtext unknown up till then (and, indeed, afterwards as well)!

Third Movement: *Scherzo. Allegro*

In this movement the unusually placed *sfz*s play an important role – another example of the rough good humour we find quite often in Beethoven. But the different meanings of the *sfz*s must then be borne in mind: in some cases they should be equated with an *f*; in others the *sfz*s often occur within a *p* phrase which is not thereby annulled. The latter occurs in **bars 7** and **15** of this movement. If one looks at the prescribed dynamic in **bar 46**, it is clear that after the last *sfz* the *p* has to be maintained to make the following *cresc.* possible. In addition, in the manuscript and in the first edition, the analogous *cresc.* in **bar 16** is missing and must undoubtedly be replaced.

The phrasing in the piano at the beginning of the movement frequently shows a recurrent bad habit, probably because of carelessness or technical inadequacy:

99

instead of

100

This would not happen if at the beginning one had a slur to the main note C and a separation of the sixteenth-note from the subsequent C.

The instruction in the first edition, *la prima parte senza repetizione*, we encounter occasionally in Beethoven, although in the Violin Sonatas it occurs only in this movement and in the *Spring* Sonata, Op. 24.

The precise execution of the dynamics called for in the violin part in **bars 22–34** makes considerable demands of bowing technique: on the one hand the short eighth-notes in **bar 26** are in *cresc.* which in *spiccato* don't quite suit the character of the passage and are more effective in *martelé* but more difficult for many violinists; on the other hand in the *p sub.* in **bar 27** one must take care that a *decresc.* in **bar 33** to the *pp* still remains possible. The triplets in the violin in **bars 29–34** should be played in *spiccato* in spite of the dots being missing, and this, I think, is also valid for **bars 16–17** and **46–47**. In the piano part I would adapt the eighth-notes of the left hand in **bars 16–17** and **46–47** to **bars 43–44** and **47** of the violin which are provided with dots; I proceed in the same way in the violin part in **bars 16–17** where the dots should be placed as they are in **46–47**.

The phrasing given in the trio – especially in the first edition, although also in the manuscript – seems rather arbitrary and imprecise. Here I follow the view presented in all subsequent editions, which looks like this:

101

Dynamically the first part, in spite of the $<>$ and *sfz*, remains in *p*.

The second part should be performed in a very distinctive manner: *p sub.* in **bar 63** but by no means *pp*, as in **bar 67** a *decresc.* follows to the real *pp* in **bar 71**.

While the quarter-notes, which have dots, can in the first violin section be played *spiccato* in *p*, let me make a plea for a strong *martelé* using lots of bow in *f* from **bar 76**.

One bad habit which appears fairly regularly is an unintended *sfz* on the last note of the violin in **bar 83** and in the piano in **bar 84**. The phrase does remain in *f* in both cases, but without accentuation.

Fourth Movement: *Finale. Allegro*

This finale shows close affinity to the first movement of the Sonata and should, both emotionally and formally, be understood as the concluding parenthesis, conferring an admirable unity on the work as a whole. Here, too, can be found the hurried breathlessness which I mentioned at the beginning of my reflections on this Sonata.

In the manuscript the dots above or below the notes are not at all uniform throughout this movement, nor are they so in the first edition; and in subsequent editions (including the

Urtext) there are conflicting interpretations. I believe that
almost all quarter-notes, as in the beginning, should have
dots, whether noted later or not. It should all be construed as
a *simile*, as it were. With **bars 13**, **105** and **178** a slight calm
comes into the music, which can be taken as the end of the
phrase; and separation from the succeeding – more lyrical –
theme seems justified. Hence I recommend here a tiny *calando*.
The dynamic of **bars 15–22**, **107–114**, and **179–182** is often
neglected by both instruments. But it should be noted here
that only in the first case (**bars 15–22**) are the specifications
exact; in the second case (**bars 107–114**) the *cresc.* in the
initial bar and the *decresc.* in **bar 113** are missing in both
instruments, as are the *sfz* and the *decresc.* in the third instance
(**bar 181**). The dynamics in **bars 43**, **47**, **61**, **205**, **209** and
223 are (in the manuscript and first edition) written irregular-
ly and imprecisely – even contradictorily. In all these cases I
favour letting the *p* in both instruments enter after, but not at,
the beginning of the bar each time. Where there are eighth-
notes in the left hand of the piano, the *p* should occur already
on the second eighth-note, but otherwise not until the second
quarter-note. The justification for my assumption is provided
by a comparison with the piano entries in **bars 48** and **210**,
which also come after the beginning of the bar. The violinist
should forego a stress on the first quarter-notes in **bars 49**,
51–52, **211** and **213–214**, for the *sfz*s are meant to alternate
between the two instruments, and the phrasing is really to be
understood as follows:

102

In **bar 63** a grace-note is specified but two bars later it is
not. The grace-note in **bar 225** is even written out in full size
with rhythmic value; but two bars later any such instruction is
absent. I propose to follow the first instance in each case, i.e.,
to attach grace-notes everywhere in both instruments. At the
second point in this case, the grace-notes, in **bar 227**, must be
executed with both B and C:

One bad habit violinists have picked up is to put an *sfz* in **bars 72** and **234**, although the temptation may seem understandable as an *fp* is written in the piano part. I find it interesting that Beethoven had originally planned an *sfz* for the violin, too, but crossed out this instruction in the manuscript; it is accordingly omitted in the first edition.

The second *p* which Beethoven wrote in **bars 77** and **239** has given rise to various interpretations: it is possible to regard the *sfz* written three bars before as an *f*, and the second *p* as a *p sub.* – which, however, would also have to apply to the second *sfz* after the second *p* – or to return again to the *p* after the *sfz* only as a restarting of the phrase. Both interpretations are justified.

The repeated notes of the violin (**bars 83–87** and **249–251**) should each have a slight individual stress, first because of the piano's right hand entries, but also in order to achieve clear rhythmical definition, which can easily turn out blurred in the concert hall when the notes are at the same pitch.

From the upbeat in **bar 115** the violin should lead up to **bar 122** while the piano only imitates, but from **bar 123**, with the upbeat, we find the opposite relationship which both partners have to take intelligently into account. A slight *ritardando* in **bar 163** is justified, I think, although not specially written.

In the last fifteen bars before the *presto* the quarter-notes in the piano should certainly not be taken too short; they are quite explicitly marked *con espressione* and without dots. The *con espressione* for the piano and *espressivo* for the violin in **bars 267–268** should not give occasion for analytical speculation: they are identical in their meaning. The difference is but further testimony to Beethoven's inattention and haste. The kind of expression required in the violin here is difficult to put into words. In this connection I refer to Beethoven's expression indication in the *Cavatina* of the String Quartet, Op. 130, where we find *beklemmt* – 'uneasy', 'oppressed'.[3] Individual

---

[3] See Translators' Note on p. 178.

instrumental realizations of this expression are bound to give differing results. To do justice to this almost uncanny passage, on the one hand through bowing division and on the other though vibrato, substantial contrasts can be obtained, both in the *Cavatina* and in this movement. A really authentic representation is actually impossible, as each clear conception finds its own instinctive reflection in inexplicable intermediate shadings. I warn both partners not to start too early with the *cresc.*, which should be effected short and steep, only from **bar 275**. The last two bars before the *presto* amount to a *morendo*, i.e., a slight *calando*.

The *presto* must begin startlingly and dramatically, with a bang. If the violinist uses bow changes in the slurs in the first four bars (which I recommend), he should do so as nearly inaudibly as possible, and thus also without cæsuras. The syncopated notes of the violin (**bars 288–295**) are, despite the *p*, to be accented slightly. The gradation of the *cresc.* to the *f* from **bar 292** deserves special attention, as does the difference between *f* in **bar 298** and *ff* in **bar 300**. Altogether the dynamic realization of the whole *presto* is uncommonly difficult if one is not prepared to compromise.

Sonata No. 8 in G major, Op. 30, No. 3

Dedicated to Emperor Alexander I of Russia
Manuscript: British Museum, London
Composed 1802
First Edition 1803

Introduction

Although I do not always find myself in agreement with Joseph Szigeti's views, especially on fingering and bowing, I believe that he succeeded admirably in the following brief description of this Sonata,[1] and it corresponds in essence with my view:

> With the Eighth Sonata we are in the realm of a kind of conflict-less perfection where the proportion and sunny gaiety of the first movement, the stately beauty of the *Tempo di Minuetto*, and the good-humoured bounce of the concluding Rondo combine to give us one of the most harmonious works of the set.

Dynamic refinements, such as the differences, very clearly marked, between *p* and *pp*, here play a major role. There are places, especially in the development of the first movement, which seem almost symphonic. With this Sonata Beethoven succeeded in achieving a happy balance, insofar as all of the thematic material is equally suitable for both instruments (an aspect of composition which achieved particular perfection with Mozart).

The question of tempo in the second movement is decidedly difficult to solve. The instructions themselves give rise to many doubts: *Tempo di Minuetto* (in the first edition with *e*:

[1] *op. cit.*, p. 28.

Menuetto) ma molto moderato (obviously added at a later date) *e grazioso*. Beethoven's rather long and somewhat repetitive heading reveals a degree of uncertainty. Now, since the composer wrote out all the repeats, in deliberate avoidance of the usual repeat signs, the movement gives the appearance of being a little too long, especially because in the re-appearance of the material we find hardly any change or variation. I therefore consider a flowing tempo suitable. The rough humour in the subsidiary theme, which starts with **bars 59** and **149** of the left hand in the piano, should by no means be smoothed out, although the violin remains unaffected by it and continues its blissful song. It is just this contrast which, with an almost dramatic effect, gives this passage its considerable appeal.

The last movement is in the composer's markedly virtuosic vein, like the C minor Sonata, Op. 30, No. 2, and, even more so, the *Kreutzer* Sonata, Op. 47. This movement is truly enchanting and spirited, full of fascinating humour and unique inventions – as, for instance, the sudden modulation in **bar 177**.

Unfortunately the dynamic instructions are extremely inexact throughout the work, frequently even contradictory, in the autograph as well as in the first edition, and an exhaustive elucidation of this whole problem, especially in this Sonata, is urgently required. Much that is missing must be supplied according to one's own view and – where there is no evidence of intended differences – adjusted according to any parallel passages.

The confusion is understandable. Beethoven himself reveals the conditions under which he is occasionally working when he writes:[2]

> I live entirely in my music; and hardly have I completed one composition when I have already begun another. At my present rate of composing, I often produce three or four works at the same time. . . .

[2] In a letter to Franz Wegeler, dated 29 June 1802. The full text of this letter, written in some distress at the onset of deafness, is quoted in Thayer, *op. cit.*, pp. 283–5. Emily Anderson, whose translation this is (*op. cit.*, pp. 57–62), dates this letter exactly a year earlier.

First Movement: *Allegro assai*

The upbeat to **bar 5** is often started in *p* because (so the argument goes) in this bar a second *f* is written. The piano has a continued *f* in **bar 4** which is valid also for the violin; the renewed *f* printed in **bar 5** serves only as confirmation that the volume intended is different from the *p* at the beginning.

The dynamics of **bars 7**, **119** and **123** in the piano are very obscure. The various editions give different pointers as to interpretation: in the Henle edition the *p* is always at the beginning of the bar; while in the Joachim edition the *p* is given once at the beginning but the second and third times not until the second eighth-note. The first edition, too, contains different markings; thus in **bar 7** there are even two *p*s, one at the beginning of the bar for the left hand, and for the right hand another *p* on the second eighth-note. In **bars 119** and **123**, on the other hand, the *p* is given very clearly on the second eighth-note, i.e., only for the right hand. In the manuscript the *p*s are written very imprecisely; and the interpretation of these places is thus an individual question. For me it is perfectly clear that **bars 7**, **119** and **123**, despite the *f* of the violin, should begin *p*. **Bar 3** shows a *cresc.* to the *f*, which is missing in **bars 7**, **119** and **123** and should be replaced. Beethoven very often writes the dynamic for one part only but he means by this an analogous application to the other parts. I am thinking here, for instance, of the *Romance* in F major, Op. 50, for violin and orchestra, where in **bars 69−71** there is a dynamic specification for the horn only, i.e., first an *fp*, then in the next bar an *f*, and finally in the subsequent bar even an *ff*. One can hardly assume that all the other instruments, including the solo violin, should remain entirely unaffected by this. Hence in **bars 12** and **128** of this Sonata the piano would have to adhere to what is specified for the violin, i.e., first a *cresc.* followed by a *p sub*.

In **bar 17**, too, in the first edition there is a *cresc.* in the violin part, but according to the manuscript and the parallel passage (**bar 135**) that should not occur until **bar 19**. The *cresc.* which is missing in the manuscript and the first edition in **bar 19** must also be made good. I do not believe however that this *cresc.* from **bar 19** can really continue over a whole thirteen bars to **bar 32**. In the analogous phrase in the recapitulation, however, it would be possible as here we are dealing with only five bars. If we go by the recapitulation the new *cresc.* should start again only in **bar 28**; for me, therefore, the first *cresc.* is arrested by the *sfz* in **bar 21**. With the exception of the *sfz*s in **bars 21**, **23** and **25** I believe more in an almost continuous *p*.

From **bar 28** on I propose a *cresc.* over four bars as is made clear from **bar 136**. **Bars 28** and **30**, as well as **136** and **138**, can be executed in *sautillé* in the violin. I do not find the trills in **bars 28−31** and **136−139** convincing without grace-notes; on the other hand the basic tempo is, after all, so fast that an extended trill plus grace-note seems very questionable; hence rather a mordent:

104

The dynamic written in **bars 35−40** differs, no doubt unintentionally, from that in **bars 143−148**. An adaptation of the first instance to **bars 143−148** seems to me musically convincing and to be recommended; in **bars 35−36**, therefore, only *p* and from **bar 37** *pp*.

Neither player should anticipate the *f* in **bars 50** and **158** but should let it enter suddenly as a *subito*. Pianists especially tend to play even the upbeat loudly. The violin trill in **bars 49** and **157** should be played similarly to **bar 28**:

105

In **bars 55−56** in the manuscript, as in the first edition, the *sfz*s in the piano part are missing. That these must be supplied is evident from **bars 163−164** in the first edition.

The dots above the last quarter-notes in **bars 57−60** and **165−168** serve again as shortenings of the note-values and in my orthography would be written outside the slur. The *sfp* in **bars 67** and **175** should be taken quite literally, although it is not too easy to do. The last eighth-notes of **bars 67–68** and **175–176** in the piano part are also to be understood as shortened by the dots. The *sfz*s of the violin in **bars 69, 73, 177** and **181** are, in my opinion, to be interpreted as soft and song-like, taking over from the last note of the piano; hence no sharp attack on the *sfz*. Despite these *sfz*s both instruments remain in *p* up to the third eighth-notes in **bars 77** and **185**.

In **bars 80** and **188** I recommend a grace-note after the violin trill. How imprecisely the grace-notes are written by Beethoven is demonstrated by **bars 92–103** and **191–196**. These are sometimes written out, and in other places they are entirely missing – even the first edition is similarly inexact. It is certain, however, that the grace-notes, written or not, are valid for the whole sequence. The *cresc.* in the *prima volta* up to the end, and with the subsequent *p sub.* in **bar 1** in the repeat, is really very difficult to execute, and a tiny rest before the *sub.* can hardly be avoided. In contrast to so many other inaccuracies, it seemed essential to Beethoven to indicate the dynamic of **bars 91–103** with extreme precision. The violinist should beware of furnishing all trills with an *sfz*; this should be done exclusively where written, and, despite the repeatedly written *p*, the pianist must not place a *cresc.* in **bars 93–94, 97–98** and **101–102** but really only where it is specifically asked for, i.e., **bars 91–92, 95–96** and **99–100**.

The left hand of the piano rumbles loudly all too often in **bars 108–113**, oblivious to the absolutely imperative *pp*, which really is necessary. This passage has an almost symphonic character, and in an orchestra it would perhaps be played by the celli. It is precisely through the *pp* that it acquires the ghostly effect intended.

Second Movement:
Tempo di Minuetto ma molto moderato e grazioso

My introduction to this Sonata referred especially to the problems of the second movement, and, indeed, some difficulties appear already in the principal theme, such as the question of *appoggiature* and grace-notes. In **bar 3** arises the question of whether the trill should have a grace-note or not. Neither in the autograph nor first edition is a grace-note written; in the manuscript the grace-note is missing each time in the theme as in **bar 6,** while in the first edition it is always present. Is the *appoggiatura* in **bar 5** to be played short or long? In the manuscript it is written in the repeats sometimes as a sixteenth-note, sometimes as an eighth-note, and occasionally left out altogether. I cannot find convincing an accumulation of very short notes and ornamental accessories in a short space of time:

106

so I would play even sixteenths in **bar 5**:

107

and of course continue in this way in the repeat of this main theme in the piano as in the violin. I hold, therefore, to the following version:

108

What today we consider a matter of course, the concurrence of ornamentation in the two instruments, was not taken quite so seriously in former times. There is a remarkable recording of this Sonata by Fritz Kreisler and Sergei Rachmaninov[3] which, for today's tastes, is interesting in many respects but no longer acceptable. In the main theme in **bar 3** Rachmaninov plays a grace-note to the trill, and the *appoggiatura* in **bar 5** he plays long:

109

[3] *The Complete Rachmaninoff*, Vol. 4, RCA Victrola AVM 3 0295 1.

Kreisler, however, uses no grace-note in **bar 11**, but plays the *appoggiatura* in **bar 13** short:

110

This differing interpretation is maintained without compromise by both artists throughout the entire movement. Either they did not notice this divergence at all (which is hardly likely), or they agreed to disagree.

Moreover, the liberties taken by both executants, especially as regards dynamics and tempi, could not be exceeded. Often *dim.*s are played in places where Beethoven expressly prescribes a *cresc*. Endings of phrases are usually supplied with a heavy *rit.*, whereby Kreisler has no scruples at employing his characteristic elegant *portato* on the mordent in the last bar of the theme. All in all, the examples mentioned are undoubtedly not the result of bad taste but reflect the spirit of the time, and for us it is of historical interest to establish this.

The *appoggiature* in **bars 19** and **23–27** should, I think, be interpreted as *acciaccature*. Whether the *cresc.* from the *pp* in **bars 29, 50, 119** and **140** should really be developed only up to the *p* of the next bar is, at the very least, doubtful. It is definitely possible – and this is my belief – that the *cresc.* is developed beyond the dynamic of this *p*, so that the next bar is probably a *p sub*.

The conspicuously opposing dynamics of the two instruments at the beginning of **bars 28, 49, 118** and **139** are unequivocally noted in the manuscript as well as in the first edition. We therefore have here a deliberate, and understandable, wish of Beethoven's with which one must comply absolutely. In addition to the many other merits of the Henle edition we find in it the helpful footnote that in very many other editions of this Sonata in **bars 40–41** and **130–131** a G is added to the piano part – on the authority neither of manuscript nor of first edition. Thus we have:

111

and not:

112

The burlesque idea of the *sfz*s in the left hand of the piano in
bars 59—65 and in the recapitulation in **bars 149—155** is very
often understated, softened, or ignored, and yet it is just the
clearly deliberate contrast to the violin theme which floats
blissfully above it that gives this passage its special charm.
The *appoggiatura* in **bars 61**, **69**, **151** and **159** I interpret as
short, i.e., to be executed in deliberate contrast to the next
bars:

113

To the violinist I recommend in **bar 74** a rather large *cresc.*
in a soft *martelé*, but he should not neglect thereby the
following *pp sub.* Whether the *cresc.* in **bar 76** is now to be only
a development from *pp* to *p*, or whether the *p* in **bar 78** is again
to be interpreted as a *p sub.* surely remains a matter of opinion.
From my understanding of the special characteristics of
Beethoven I rather tend to an earlier increase of volume,
followed by a *p sub.* The creation of contrast in the violin part
in **bars 78—85** by varied bowing styles seems to me especially
attractive. For **bar 78** I again use a soft *martelé* as in **bar 74**,
and from **bar 79** a not-too-short *spiccato*. The length of the
appoggiatura in **bars 76** and **80** is also controversial. Although
Beethoven's notation of *appoggiature* was not nearly as precise
as Mozart's, it is striking that here the *appoggiatura* was written
as an eighth-note and not – as so often – as a sixteenth-note.
The following execution is therefore possible:

114

I must admit that I myself prefer it short.

The *rit.* in the piano part in **bars 176–177**, which is
specified rhythmicly through a graded series of sixteenth-
notes, eighth-note triplets, and eighth-notes, would sound too
pedantic if one kept rigidly to the rhythm; I therefore recommend imperceptible transition.

The precisely noted dynamic from **bar 172** to the end of the movement is very characteristic of Beethoven and should be conveyed to the listener in an almost exaggerated manner.

As usual, it is appropriate to shorten the quarter-notes which have dots, here in **bars 191–195**. An *accelerando* starting with **bar 193** which may often arise as a result of the *cresc.* betrays a lack of self-control, which must be avoided, although a tiny *calando* in the last two bars is almost unavoidable.

This movement is basically finished with the first quarter-note of **bar 190**, and the continuation is only an epilogue.

Third Movement: *Allegro vivace*

The 'bagpipe' effect, which Béla Bartók and others described in this movement,[4] gains its particular attractiveness through its playful, humorous and virtuoso element. It must be performed *leggiermente*, and indeed is specifically so noted by the composer, i.e., with grace and lightness.

Let me expressly point to the phrasing which here is quite precisely specified, as in the main theme with the deliberate contrast of separated and tied sixteenth-notes, which one must bring out in performance. For the violinist this presents less of a problem than for the pianist, as the separate notes of the violin part performed in *sautillé* can sound very elegant and, in fact, shortened, while the *staccato* notes at high speed on the piano are difficult to realize.

Joseph Szigeti proposed[5] to facilitate the bowing and string-crossing for the violinist in the rondo theme through a rather tricky fingering, although I consider this unnecessary. He advises (the upper fingering is Szigeti's and the lower mine):

115

The A at the end of the first and third bars of the theme I play with different fingerings, the first time on the open string and

[4] See Szigeti, *op. cit.*, p. 29.
[5] *ibid.*, p. 51.

the second time, because of the natural string crossing, with the fourth finger. The grace-notes of the many trills are written very carelessly and imprecisely in this movement. There are also slight differences between the manuscript and the first edition, but one may assume with a likelihood bordering almost on certainty that nearly all trills should have a grace-note. Perhaps the only exceptions are the two trills in **bars 61** and **63** in the piano, which are at least conceivable without them. Most of the trills with grace-notes should, in very fast tempo, be executed thus:

116

In this figure the violinist is advised to play the first three eighth-notes with three repeated upbows, but with jumpy bowing. All *appoggiature* which occur in this movement are undoubtedly meant to be short. In **bars 20–24** one should make clear which of the two instruments has the upper voice and which the lower. Hence my proposal:

117

However, the apportioning of the voices is just the opposite in **bars 28–32**.

The trills at the end of **bars 25**, **27**, **33** and **35** should be:

118

To underline its character, which strikes one almost as Austrian, the secondary theme, which begins with the upbeat in **bar 56**, may be taken a tiny bit slower than the basic tempo of the movement. None of the *sfz*s in **bars 92–100** annul the prevailing *p*, and by attention to this dynamic one produces an even more striking effect, as the sudden outbreak of *ff* in **bar 101** occurs really unexpectedly. This *ff* is to be maintained, despite the many *sfz*s in the violin part, undiminished up to **bar 123**.

The detailed dynamic notations in **bars 123–141** should be followed most meticulously, for they are of subtle delicacy, interesting and carefully conceived.

In **bar 165** we find a *p sub.* which is not too easy to play; for both instruments a very short cæsura may be recommended for technical as well as acoustic reasons, although the violinist who goes from an *f détaché* to a *p sautillé* has a somewhat easier task.

The unconventional fingering invented by Szigeti[6] – and which delighted Bartók – in **bars 167–174** is one I find really first-rate, though not easy to play:

119

Crazy, but magnificent!

I prefer **bar 175** without any *rit.* up to the *fermata*.

The unexpected and inspired modulation to E flat major never fails to delight me anew nor in its effect on the audience. The phrasing of the beginning is slightly changed here; where previously a slur over four notes is unequivocally expected, here in **bars 181**, **183**, **185** and **187** the slurs are over two notes only.

The bizarre dynamic in **bars 192–202** borders on the technically impossible. But though grotesque and humorous, it is entirely meaningful and absolutely playable. All trills here could also have grace-notes. We find in all editions, including the first, a *p* on the first eighth-note of **bar 202** in the piano. This is not really plausible, for in the autograph it is between

---

[6] *ibid.*, p. 29.

the first and second eighth-notes; accordingly I believe one could delay the *p* until the second eighth-note.

When taking over the offbeat octave D eighth-note from the piano in **bar 206** the violinist should adjust its length (or rather, shortness) to that of the piano.

The *cresc.* in **bar 218** is very effective when begun almost in *pp*. I would maintain the tempo up to the very end without any *ritardando*, entirely in keeping with the character of this movement and its triumphant conclusion.

Sonata No. 9 in A major, Op. 47
(*Kreutzer* Sonata)

SONATA

per il Piano-forte ed un Violino obligato,

scritta in uno stile molto concertante,

quasi come d'un concerto.

Composta e dedicata al suo amico

R. KREUZER.

Membro del Conservatorio di Musica in Parigi

Primo Violino dell'Academia delle Arti, e della Camera imperiale.

per

L. van BEETHOVEN.

Opera 47.
Prezzo 6 Fr:

À BONN CHEZ N. SIMROCK.

À PARIS chez H.Simrock, professeur, marchand de musique et d'instrumens, rue du Mont Blanc N°379, Chaussée d'Antin prez le Boulevard.
Proprieté de l'éditeur.   Deposée à la Bibliothèque nationale.

**Dedicated to Rodolphe Kreutzer
Manuscript missing (the first part of the first movement
was found a few years ago and is in the
Beethoven Archives, Bonn)
Composed 1802–03
First edition April 1805**

Introduction

This Sonata occupies a very special place, and not only within
the works of Beethoven. A concerto for only two instruments,
one which does not involve any other instrument, is unique in
music. The closest 'competitors' are Weber's *Grand Duo* for
clarinet and piano, and Schubert's C major *Fantasie*, D. 934,

Rodolphe Kreutzer
16 November 1766–7 January 1831

Outstanding French violinist and composer, and an important teacher of the violin. On tour accompanying the envoy Bernadotte, he got to know Beethoven in Vienna in 1798. The work which has kept Kreutzer's name to the fore as a composer in his *Études ou Caprices* for solo violin (from around 1807), which belong among the principal teaching pieces for violinists. It was in 1805 that Beethoven dedicated to him the A major Violin Sonata, Op. 47. On 4 October 1804 Beethoven wrote to Simrock:

> This *Kreutzer* is a dear kind fellow who during his stay in Vienna gave me a great deal of pleasure. I prefer his modesty and natural behaviour to *all the exterior* without *any interior*, which is *characteristic* of the most virtuosi.

Anderson (ed.), *op. cit.*, p. 120

for violin and piano; and true, there are other works, such as the Concerto for violin and piano by the youthful Felix Mendelssohn, although this has an orchestral accompaniment. There is, too, the *Chamber Concerto* by Alban Berg, which includes parts for wind instruments, and the Concerto for violin, piano and string quartet by Ernest Chausson. There are also duos for homogeneous and heterogeneous instruments, but a concerto for two solo instruments without orchestra is exceptional. The *Kreutzer* Sonata breaks many of the rules of chamber music sonatas, and the fact that we are dealing with a concerto is already apparent in Beethoven's original title: *Sonata per il Piano-forte ed un Violino obligato, scritta in uno stile molto concertante, quasi come d'un concerto.* Furthermore, in the first edition, at the head of the violin and piano parts is the note: *Grande Sonate.*

The work was originally dedicated to the mulatto violinist George Augustus Polgreen Bridgetower who was a distinguished violinist of Beethoven's day. Later, because of a quarrel, allegedly over a girl, this dedication was changed in favour of Rodolphe Kreutzer, who detested Beethoven's works. Kreutzer did not at all appreciate this esteem, nor did he ever perform this work. Hector Berlioz writes in his *Voyage Musical en Allemagne et Italie*:[1]

> C'est à Kreutzer que Beethoven venait de dédier l'une des plus sublimes Sonates pour Pianoforte et Violon; il faut convenir que l'hommage était bien adressé. Aussi le célèbre Violon ne put-il jamais se décider à jouer cette composition outrageusement inintelligible.

Changes of dedication occurred not infrequently with Beethoven – the best-known example is the *Eroica* Symphony.

Perhaps here I may recall the original jocular dedication to Bridgetower which is to be found only in the newly discovered first part of the manuscript: *Sonata mulattica composta per il Mulatto Brischdauer gran pazzo e compositore mulattico.* When Beethoven used a foreign language, such as Italian, for example, we frequently find other spelling errors. Here he

---

[1] Labitte, Paris, 1844; reprinted by Gregg International Publisher, Farnborough, Hampshire, 1970, Vol. 1, p. 264.

spelled the name 'Bridgetower' phonetically, approximately according to his German pronunciation.

The premiere of this work is supposed to have taken place on 24 May 1803, played by Beethoven and Bridgetower themselves.

I should also like to point out that the last movement of the *Kreutzer* Sonata was originally planned as the last movement of the Sonata, Op. 30, No. 1. With the exchange of this movement (also in A major) Beethoven created a comprehensible balance to the first movement of the *Kreutzer* Sonata.

That Beethoven designated this Sonata not for 'violin and piano' but for 'piano and violin' may hardly flatter the vanity of the violinist, although the priorities occasionally seem to overlap, for from the titles of the manuscripts and of the original edition of the *Kreutzer* Sonata it can clearly be seen that Beethoven (perhaps even primarily) was thinking of the violinist. And both dedications, after all, were to violinists: Bridgetower and Kreutzer.

First Movement: *Adagio sostenuto – Presto*

The indication *Sostenuto* is missing in the manuscript.

For most violinists this unaccompanied beginning seems a nightmare. A rendition which is truly persuasive in its interpretation demands here enormous concentration and inner calm: like a prologue, it immediately proclaims a great work; indeed, it must announce the necessary atmosphere already with the very first chord. There are immediately problems with the voice-leading in **bar 2**. In fact, the original slurs should be regarded only as phrasing, for the maintaining of the slurs over the respective bars without bow changes would pose problems of sound production which would be difficult to solve. If the violinist were to take a half-way normal fingering and bowing, the voice-leading in the second bar would be misleading, thus:

George Augustus Polgreen Bridgetower
1779–1860

It was for this famous mulatto violinist that Beethoven wrote the first two movements of the Sonata, Op. 47, later dedicated to Kreutzer. The last movement was already to hand, having been composed for the A major Sonata, Op. 30, No. 1. Beethoven was much impressed by Bridgetower's lively style:

His playing in public and private at Dresden had secured him such favorable letters of introduction as gained him a most brilliant reception in the highest musical circles of the Austrian capital. . . . Beethoven, to whom he was introduced by Prince Lichnowsky, readily gave him aid in a public concert.

Thayer, op. cit., p. 333

One way out would be to start the second bar immediately on
the D and G strings, i.e., in the fifth position, the sound of
which is usually not satisfactory. There are three solutions:

121   1.

122   2.

123   3.

All three versions require changes of bow which need by no
means detract from the total character of the phrasing,
provided that the violinist can command a good (i.e., inaudible) bow change.

The first chord is best broken by playing the G and D
strings first alone, for in the continuation it is simply a matter
of two parts, i.e., double stopping. Furthermore, a very slow
tempo must be chosen, so that actually on the first quarter-
note only a strong *f* with a *dim.* can be played. The spreading
of the chords in **bars 3** and **4** can be executed either two and
two, or one and two. In order to hold the chords in *p*, breaking
is unfortunately unavoidable.

I regard it as undisciplined, even unmusical, when pianists
start from **bar 5** in a completely different tempo than that just
used by the violinist. One should agree beforehand on the
common tempo, but if the violinist, from whim or nervous-
ness, starts off with a different tempo from the one agreed on,
the pianist cannot, with finger raised, as it were admonishing-
ly indicate: 'This is how it must be!' Beyond this, the entry of
the piano in this particular bar often comes too early and

precipitately. The very rest between the ending of the violin phrase and the entry of the piano is of pregnant significance. How easily the atmosphere of this prologue can be upset right at the beginning!

The change of one leading instrument to the other in **bars 8–11** must be accomplished very precisely; to provide the descending phrasing of the piano in **bars 8** and **10** with a *dim.* is of equal importance to the almost inaudible entry of the violin. A well-distributed *crescendo* of both instruments is advisable if only because violinists in particular like to play even the first chord in *ff.* Although in the violin part the chord in **bar 9** is written in four voices to the end, one can hold only the C on the A string as long as the main voice on the E string.

Incidentally, the manuscript only gives very few dynamic indications in the *Adagio* introduction, which, in the form we know, were obviously added later, in the first edition. Among these is the dot in the piano part on the first eighth-note in **bars 14–17** which is missing in the violin part. It is my opinion that the shortening of the note-value of these eighth-notes by the dots is valid also for the violin, so that for both instruments the first eighth-note also of each bar mentioned is practically a sixteenth-note (like all the other notes). In **bar 17** the *decresc.* of the violin should be made on the last somewhat lengthened sixteenth-note, and not before.

At the end of the introduction one often cannot hear the violin any more; but the A in the piano must die away together with the F of the violin as a third, and also end at the same time. For this a planned bow division is necessary.

At the beginning of the *Presto* the violinist can play either a *martelé* at the point of the bow or a *spiccato* (thrown bow) at the nut. I myself prefer *martele*, a method of bowing which – as I have said – is becoming less and less fashionable. In any case, the violinist would find it advantageous to choose a fingering which makes it possible to bring out the two voices, and in this case to play the second and third quarter-notes of **bars 20–24** and **31–33** on a lower string.

In **bar 26** the note-values are differently written in the manuscript and in the first edition. In the manuscript we have:

124

In the first edition we find:

125

With normal fingering, playing the E (with its *fermata*) on the open string is unavoidable. In the two preceding bars one naturally uses vibrato, so that the open E string, suddenly without vibrato, does not provide acoustic continuity and also brings with it, with the popular steel strings, a stridency which is not entirely pleasant.

I myself therefore choose a fingering which reproduces the version of the first edition more exactly:

126

as the breaking of the chord and the shortening of the three lower notes are clearly apparent from Beethoven's notation. Even in the first printing this notation is used clearly in the recapitulation in **bars 351−352** and **357**:

127

The violinist should remain aware that though he has the leading voice in **bars 19−27**, **bars 28−36** belong to the piano; the violin here plays the secondary voice. The piano cadenza in **bar 36** is to be executed with complete freedom. I consider wrong the habit some pianists have of bringing in the last C in the bass very late; under the note E in the right hand, which has a *fermata*, there is only an eighth-note rest in the bass; and the *fermata* in the left hand is not on the rest but on the eighth-note C.

Out of interest, let me point out further that in the manuscript the *arpeggio* of the cadenza is not written out – it consists only of the chord:

128

The slurs in the violin part are entirely different in the manuscript, in the first edition and in later ones. In the first edition the slur begins with the upbeat to **bar 37** and does not stop until **bar 41**.

First edition:

129

Manuscript:

130

Joachim edition:

131

Henle edition:

132

To me the phrasing in the manuscript makes most sense, first, because it continues the beginning of the *Presto*, as it were, and secondly, as it is also reconfirmed in **bars 335–344**.

The dynamic in **bars 45** and **366** has given occasion to the most differing interpretations in all editions. In **bar 45** Joseph Joachim writes the *p* on the first note of the bar, but in **bar 366** on the second eighth-note. In Henle the *p* is at the beginning of the bar both times but only in the pianist's copy; in the separate violin copy the *p* is on the first eighth-note the first time and on the second eighth-note in **bar 366**. The first edition, in the piano copy, shows the *p* at the beginning of **bar**

45, but in **bar 366** on the second eighth-note. In the separate violin copy of the same edition we find the *p* both times on the second eighth-note.

Other interpreters have thought of yet further possibilities! I prefer the *p* not until the second eighth-note.

Dynamic differentiation of the two instruments in **bars 45–60** and **366–381** seems indispensable to me, for with every two-bar phrase the main weight is transferred from one instrument to the other. Here the division between a leading and an accompanying voice should be clearly defined. For the violinist there arises the question of whether he prefers to play these bars in *sautillé* or *détaché*. The clear separation of the eighth-notes which results from a jumpy bow can hardly be executed on the piano at the required speed. Although a jumpy bowing is attractive for the eighth-notes, personal taste must decide whether to play their length as in or in contrast to the piano. The manuscript contains hardly any dynamic specifications; the ornamentation, too, is largely omitted. In the first edition, on the other hand, we find quite detailed instructions on both aspects.

The many *sfz*s from **bar 61** and from **bar 382** on, in the two parts, should be followed exactly; but, equally, none may be added.

How can the *f*-chords be distinguished from those which are given an additional *sfz*? I would propose to hold these *sfz* chords a little longer than the others.

As I have mentioned, in **bars 75–76** and **79–80** there are no grace-notes written in the manuscript, but in the first edition they are noted, with a single exception.

Of the parallel passages in **bars 396–397** and **400–401**, one can say only that the grace-notes are recorded also in the first edition, although, unfortunately, it is not possible to check with the manuscript because the second part is missing. At any rate, the phrasing in the manuscript is at variance with that in the first edition.

133   In the manuscript we find:

In the first edition:

134

while most other editions recommend the following:

135

I myself tie the grace-notes to the trills but use a fresh bow for the following quarter-note.

The violin *sfz*s in **bars 81–88** can be considerably strengthened in the first four bars by involving the open E string:

136

The last bar before the lyrical secondary theme (**bars 90** and **411**) presents a very interesting variant in the piano which most pianists nonetheless overlook. The second time round (in **bar 411**) the E in the left hand must – in contrast to its previous occurrence – be sounded again.

Bars 89–90:

137

Bars 410–411:

138

The question of whether in **bars 95** and **416** the mordent in the violin part should have, as in the piano, a semitone for the lower interval (as noted by Joachim, for example) or, as a contrast, have a whole-tone interval, will probably remain an eternal issue. In any case, it should be noted that the violin has to play this theme in the major both times, while the piano is in the minor. Moreover, in the very sketchy manuscript the mordents are missing altogether, but in the separate violin copy of the first edition we find the first time, in **bar 95**:

139    and in **bar 416**:    140

The sharp sign above and below the mordent must, I suppose, be a printing error, for it cannot have meant the following:

141

But if it were meant as a double sharp it would look like this:

142

and hence only a semitone after all. In addition we have the sharp above the mordent in **bar 416**. No D sharp can have been intended by this:

143

Such notations are always imprecise with Beethoven, for he did not spend time on noting the differences between a sharp above or below a mordent or trill. Thus there remains again the possibility of a semitone for the lower interval, that is, B sharp:

144

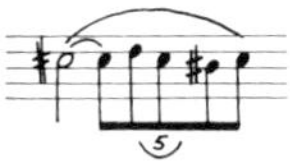

Such an authority as the late Joseph Schmidt-Görg was convinced[2] that there must be a whole-tone interval in both cases, while I myself still have doubts, for the reasons mentioned above. (I bring this issue up here only for discussion without wanting to take a firm stance one way or the other).

[2] In a letter to Günter Henle.

Neither in the piano nor in the violin would I play the mordent rhythmically in the usual way:

because Beethoven could have written it out so if he had wished, let alone because it is after all pedantic and dry, and no longer to be regarded as an ornament (the second half of the bar is better as a quintuplet).

The *cresc.* in the piano in **bars 115** and **436** should, of course, be taken as utopian and only as an indication of expressive intent; but in order to help realize this idea better, some details should be considered: the violinist should, in any case, play a proper *cresc.* with subsequent *p sub.*, and the pianist, for his part, should play **bars 115** and **436** not too quietly, and play the *arpeggio* in the next bar very nearly *pp*. Furthermore, one must consider whether the pianist should start the *arpeggio* with left and right hands simultaneously or proceed from low to high. Similarly, the question arises of whether the violinist should begin the *p sub.* together with the first bass note of the piano or wait with his entry for the top note of the *arpeggio*? In my opinion, the entry of the violin in **bars 116** and **437** belongs on the first bass note of the piano *arpeggio*. Although the dyamic in the first edition in **bars 120** and **441** in the piano is self-contradictory, as in later editions, I concur with the view of the Henle editor, Sieghard Brandenburg, who does not let the *p* begin – as in the violin part – until the last quarter-note. In the first edition in **bar 120** the *p* is written on the third quarter-note, and in the parallel passage it does not come until **bar 442**. In Joachim, for instance, these *p*s are found already on the second quarter-note. But in the manuscript there is again no indication.

I should like to point out the rhythmic differentiation of the violin part in **bars 129–130** and **450–451**: the first time it is with rests, the second time without. I do not look on this difference as carelessness precisely because it is found also in the piano part in **bars 133–134** and **454–455**!

To bring out the upbeat of the piano clearly in **bars 143** and **464**, a tiny *rallentando* is recommended. The left hand of the piano in this theme (**bars 144** and **465**) is often played too softly, sometimes even with pedalling. A hard, terse and very rhythmic *staccato* would be more suitable to its character.

The *pizz.* in **bars 149–155** and **469–476** are to be played as strongly as possible. In the trills in **bars 151**, **163**, **217**, **221**, **224–225**, **472**, and **484**, I consider a grace-note necessary. In **bars 147**, **159**, **197**, **205**, **213**, **228**, **232**, **236**, **261**, **468** and **480** I usually shorten all quarter-notes, whether so printed or not. In this connection I should like to point to the secondary theme in **bar 144** and its various repetitions, to the rhythmic precision which is also evident in the development (**bars 226–228**, **230–232** and **234–236**): in the theme itself it is three times long and twice short, but in the development twice long and once short. In **bars 168** and **489** a very slight *dim.* after the *sfz* is advisable for both instruments so that the following *cresc.* to the *ff* becomes clearly discernible. There is a problem of balance between violin and piano posed in **bars 178–179** as in **182–190** and in the parallel passages, **bars 499–500** and **503–517**. If the piano plays the chords inconsiderately in *ff* (maybe even with pedal), the violinist can then merely be seen but no longer heard. (How much of a loss this is depends very much on the appearance of the violinist!) On the other hand, too soft a chord in the piano would amount to a falsification of the character of this passage. I therefore propose that the pianist play the chords with a clear conscience as vehemently and as *ff* as he wants to but extremely short, because in this way the violin gets its due during the piano rests.

Whether such bowings as those in **bars 188–189** and **210–225** should be taken seriously is very questionable, for they are not at all violinistic and give little tonal satisfaction. I believe the violinist should not succumb too much here to 'Urtext snobbery' and should so arrange his bowings and slurs that a maximum of volume and of beauty of sound is reached. My own version looks like this:

146   **bar 188:**

whereby the piano does not enter with its chord in **bar 190** until the top D of the violin.

Bar 210–225:

The dynamic written in **bars 201–202** and **257–258** is somewhat utopian if the piano actually maintains the *ff* into the beginning of the next bar, and if the *p* which is written for the upbeat of the violin is followed to the letter. As the entries of the violin represent, after all, the secondary theme it would be nonsense to drown them out. We have to seek a way out here: either in **bars 201** and **257** the piano must make a *dim.* to lead to the *p*, or the violin should start not quite in *p*, perhaps *mf* with an immediate *dim.* Both alternatives are feasible, although I prefer the second. In **bars 242–245** of the violin and **246–249** of the piano the quarter-notes should be shortened, just as are the endings of **bars 228, 232, 236** and **240**. The *sfz*s in **bars 270–273** are not, for me, identical with *f*, hence my version: accentuation of the *sfz*s and everything else in *p*.

Phrasing and dynamic in both instruments in **bars 274–277** and **282–285** are often misunderstood and executed wrongly. For one thing, the *p* notation on the first eighth-note of the violin in **bar 274** makes no sense, for not only does the phrase here begin on the second eighth-note, but the piano also has the *p* properly after the first beat. Moreover, in the first edition a relevant dynamic notation is missing for the violin in **bar 282**, from which it is clearly evident that the first E flat ends the preceding phrase, and the second one, similar to **bar 274**, is the beginning of the next one. For the rest, generally, the only correct phrasing of both instruments in

bars 274–293 is grossly neglected. For me, **bars 274–275** and **282–283** each constitute one-bar phrases but **bars 276–277** and **284–285** are two-bar phrases. The left hand in the piano should therefore be:

148

The same applies to **bars 282–286**. In these bars the violin would therefore have to phrase as follows:

149

The *dim.* which can often be heard in **bars 309** and **319** is surely wrong, for there is no *legato* until after the *p sub.* and a *decresc.* follows in both cases. The only exception to this is the *fp* in the violin in **bar 308**.

In **bars 406–409** the violinist can help the *sfz* on the E effectively by playing the open E string at the same time. It is a matter for debate whether the right hand in the piano part in **bar 478** should really play an E on the first eighth-note – as printed in all editions – for an A as in bars preceding and following would make more sense (compare also **bar 157**). Both partners should beware of taking the *p* (for the violin in **bar 517** and for the piano **bar 518**) too literally, and should consider that from **bar 521** there is still a *dim.* to come which does not lead to *pp* until **bar 523**. In the first printing of the violin part the *sfz*s are without exception on the last quarter-notes of **bars 539–541** instead of on the third quarter-note as in the piano, which in my opinion is a printing error.

The fact that in the piano the pedal sign already begins at **bar 561** – which, with the quarter-note rests also noted, would sound just like the following bars – is probably because of the nature of the piano in Beethoven's day.

In most editions (including the first) the *Adagio* marked in the piano does not come until **bar 575**, while for the violin the *Adagio* starts already in **bar 574** – as an upbeat. The marking in the violin seems the more logical, as Beethoven writes the *Adagio* also on the same upbeat in the piano (**bar 578**). I do not therefore find convincing the comfortable solution of allowing both instruments to delay the beginning of the *Adagio* until **bar 575**. My proposal is to put a *rit.* on **bars 573–574** in the piano, which leads logically to the *Adagio*. To keep the *Presto* in the piano up to the end of **bar 574** while the violinist begins his upbeat in *Adagio* is unthinkable; moreover, the subsequent *Tempo I* also starts with the upbeat.

The piano dynamic Beethoven noted for **bar 579** is again utopian and certainly cannot be played as the preceding bars of the violin were. All that the pianist can do is to play the chord in the next bar a little stronger.

The partners should not let themselves be carried away and reach their limit of tonal volume already at **bar 583**, for the last four bars should sound as a clear intensification towards the *ff* – the preceding bars have only an *f*.

Second Movement: *Andante con Variazioni*

The tempi of the theme and variations have always been very controversial. Although I do not share the idea of playing the whole movement in one and the same tempo, I do consider an approximation of the speeds of the theme and variations to be desirable. I have often witnessed interpretations in which the theme was performed as a tragic *adagio*, and when the first variation was reached the pianist opened up with a considerably faster tempo, whereupon the violinist played 'his' second variation *prestissimo*!

Eye- and ear-witnesses have passed down to us the impressions of a concert with Pablo de Sarasate, who played this violin variation in a racing tempo (which, on the basis of his recording of the Prelude from Bach's Third Partita, I can well imagine), then bowed and, in response to the frantic applause of the audience, repeated the entire variation!

Most of the time the partners calm down noticeably in the third variation, only to play again a faster tempo in the fourth. The *Tempo I* which follows the *Molto Adagio* is then played

according to the original slow tempo of the theme. I am of the
opinion that the total character of this second movement
should, rather, be understood as fluid, if only because of the
original marking of *Andante*. Except for the *Molto Adagio* in **bar
192** and the subsequent *Tempo I*, no changes of tempo are
prescribed.

My proposal is to choose not too rigid a speed nor over-wild
differences in tempo. I prefer the theme lightly flowing,
graceful, Variations I and II (if only because of the intended
virtuosity) a little faster, and III and IV in approximately the
same speed as the theme.

And now to details: I think it essential to recognize here
what happens to the form of the theme. The first eight bars are
devoted to the first part of the theme, which is first introduced
by the piano and repeated by the violin in the following eight
bars. From **bar 17** – with preceding upbeat – the piano
continues the second part of the theme, and this section is
eventually concluded in the piano with the repetition of the
first part (**bars 28–35**). **Bars 28–35** should therefore be
played by the violin with rather more restraint than **bars
9–16** and **36–54**. From **bar 36** the violin takes the lead again
by continuing the second part of the theme (as had the piano
in **bars 17–35**), and also closing with a repetition of the first
part. As most violinists play **bars 28–35** in the same soloistic
and leading manner as **bars 9–16** and **47–54** I am keen that
this error be rectified.

The grace-notes in this theme are interpreted very differently. Urtext purists don't allow any grace-note where it isn't
written, but go so far in this respect that, for instance, they
consider that grace-notes written in the violin part in **bar 45**,
and in the piano with exactly the same thematic procedure in
bar 26, should not be used – further demonstration that even
an Urtext must be considered critically. A grace-note in **bars
7**, **15**, **34** and **53** is entirely permissible but not mandatory.
On the other hand, leaving out the grace-notes in the piano in
bar 26 is certainly an omission which ought to be corrected.

In this theme, too, there is a very exact dynamic notation by
the composer which, unfortunately, both instrumentalists
quite often neglect. The *cresc.* in **bar 4** and the following *p sub.*

must be taken really seriously. The same holds true for all parallel passages, which underlines its significance, for otherwise Beethoven would not have pointed it out anew in each case. In **bars 15** and **53** the $\diagup$ written in **bars 7** and **34** is missing and should be supplied. Similarly in the piano the *cresc.* in **bars 24** and **25**, which is given quite clearly in the same place in the violin in **bars 43** and **44**, is missing. The *p* in **bar 26** should make no sense without this *cresc.*

A comparison of **bars 30** and **49** is interesting, as in the first case no trill is written in the left hand of the piano but is found even in the first edition in the repetition in **bar 49**. Is this difference intentional or should it be judged a sin of omission? I am against an adjustment here, for in **bar 49** in both instruments – but also in the two preceding bars of the violin – *appoggiature* are given, i.e., ornamentation which we have not met before. The trill in the piano which occurs only in **bar 49** would accordingly be a part of the ornamentation.

The pianist would do well to delay starting the first chord of **bar 47** until the main note E of the violin, so that the violinist has time to play his *appoggiatura* after the very short thirty-second-note of the preceding bar. In **bars 7–8**, **15–16**, **27** and **34–35** the rather large *ritardandi* which one hears so often are, in my opinion, unnecessary: they distort the flow and are not too clever when repeated five times within a short time-span. I could understand a slight *ritardando* in **bar 46** and right at the end of the theme (**bars 53–54**).

Variation I

In this quasi-piano-solo variation one could make certain dynamic supplementations which, adjusted to the theme, are musically entirely plausible, such as (for instance) an *sfz* on the second triplet in **bar 65**, a *cresc.* in **bar 66**, and an *sfz* on the third triplet in **bar 67**. As a general principle one returns to the *p* again after every *sfz*. I also approve of grace-notes after the trills in the upbeat and on the last eighth-note in **bars 55** and **74**.

Whatever dynamic is chosen in the piano, the violin should not go along with it. The expressly marked *sempre piano* should be a clear pointer here. On the other hand, it is a matter of course to adjust the timing of the violinist to the piano. The slight *rit.* usual in **bar 73** corresponds to the parallel passage in the theme in **bar 46**, in the second variation in **bar 100** and in the third variation in **bar 127**.

The *legato* notes in **bars 68–69** often stand in insufficient constrast to their *staccato* surroundings; this is caused by careless pedalling.

The *rit.* at the end of every section and over-long rests between the variations are, I feel, superfluous and quite disturb the total continuity.

Variation II

In the original edition the piano basses are written as sixteenth-notes with rests, right from the beginning, as in the whole variation with the exception of **bars 94–96**; this is in contrast to almost all printed editions which have eighth-notes for the first four bars plus upbeat. The original notation is more plausible and makes the dots below the eighth-notes unnecessary.

This virtuoso violin variation can be played with various bowings: either every third and fourth note separately up and down, starting with ⊓ or ∨ :

150

or:

151

or indeed:

152

I prefer this last (probably most unusual) bowing which I myself and my students (and now, too, my 'violin grandchildren') like to use also in other works. Thus it has come about in the course of time that this type of bowing became associated with myself and has entered the world of violinists as 'Rostal bowing'.

Each of the alternatives mentioned above is acceptable, but certainly not an up-and-down *détaché*, which in no way does justice to the character and the marking *leggiermente*. Regrettably, the *détaché* is used occasionally. When no slur occurs, a *sautillé* is appropriate, but when the slight *rit.* mentioned occurs (as in **bar 100**) this can develop into a controlled *spiccato*. The violinist should consider when choosing his dynamic that in **bar 97** there is a sudden *pp*. He should also carefully observe *cresc.* and *p sub.*

This variation seduces those who are technically very able to a very fast virtuoso tempo which may be aesthetically dubious – and, in connection with the whole movement, perhaps even a bit vulgar! As I mentioned in connection with Variation I, I advise against *rit.* with the exception of **bar 100** and the end of the variation.

Variation III *Minore*

It is astonishing how many pianists make a *cresc.* already in **bar 113** and **132** which is not justified until the next bar. Here the violinist is less prone to yield to temptation because of the *fp* expressly noted. My advice tends rather towards providing these places with a *dim.* in the piano part. If one plays all the repeats in this variation the ending occurs unchanged no less than four times; hence I warn anew against too many *ritardandi*. The dynamic which here is again noted quite precisely should be observed as faithfully as possible, as should the sudden *sfz* in **bar 126**. Unfortunately the *sfz* is often wrongly applied also to the second eighth-note of **bar 127** where a slowly-rising *cresc.* is provided for. The violinist should know that at the end of **bar 121** the piano still has to play a thirty-second-note in the right hand after the last sixteenth-note, which means a very slight drawing-out before the *p sub.* in the next bar but no shortening of the last note.

In **bars 123–124** in the violin part the natural signs are missing in the first editions, but in all subsequent ones the appropriate correction is made.

Variation IV *Maggiore*

The basic character of this variation is similar to that of the
theme: graceful, lightly flowing, playful, almost like a 'musical
box'. The *dim.*s which are written in many editions (including
Joachim's) in **bars 143** and **151** do not correspond to the
original edition. Thus the *cresc.* rises in both cases definitely up
to the *p sub.* It is missing in the piano part in **bar 142**, as it is in
bars 150 and **169**. In the violin the *cresc.* is missing in **bar 142**
(compare **bar 169**).

The violinist faces certain problems in the execution of an
acoustically satisfying *pizzicato*. This is mostly a matter of high
notes on the E string. As is well-known, such *pizzicati* often
sound rather wretched in comparison to those of a viola or
cello. Very firmly pressed fingers of the left hand and a good
choice of contact point (e.g., closer to the bridge) can be very
helpful.

The differentiated notation of the piano and violin parts in
the main theme is worthy of note. The mordent in **bar 136** is
not written out – in contrast to the violin part (**bars 144** and
182) – but it amounts to the same thing. A calm rendition, not
too fast, is to be recommended – perhaps something like this:

153

It is not quite clear, furthermore, why in the same theme of
the violin in **bar 144** the ornamentation at the beginning of
the bar is missing, for the first four bars are otherwise nearly
identical with the piano part. In the case of the trills,
grace-notes should be used only where they are expressly
asked for. **Bar 140** provides for a grace-note which, however,
is missing in the repetition in **bar 167**: an adaptation seems
imperative.

The phrasing in **bars 151–153** and **170–172** is interpreted
very differently, either as:

154

or:

155

Something may be said for both versions: though the first appears attractive, the second would be more correct. The slurs and dots above the eighth-notes are written very carelessly: it is absolutely necessary to create agreement here. The grace-note in **bar 181** of the violin is, rhythmicly, not easily managed; as we are dealing with a similar small *rit.* to that in **bars 46**, **73**, **100** and **127** I would distribute the notes as follows:

156

The unexpected and extremely beautiful modulation on the last eighth-note of **bar 183** is an inspiration which deserves special attention; hence my recommendation of a slight *espressivo* on the F sharp in the left hand of the piano.

Very many violinists tend to start the *cresc.*, which should not commence until **bar 188**, considerably earlier, which rather detracts from its sweetness, tenderness and elegance.

However the tempo of this variation turns out, **bar 190** in the piano must correspond to the *Tempo I* of **bar 194**. The *Tempo I* signals only the annulment of the preceding *molto adagio*.

The use of pedals in **bars 192–193**, which is also written in the first edition, I do not find particularly beautiful on our modern grand pianos. The effect was obviously a completely different one on a grand piano of Beethoven's day. My proposal – to use the middle pedal on today's Steinway grand so as to maintain in this way the bass note D without all those held notes producing unattractive dissonances at the same time – is rejected by all pianists, without exception! They prefer such compromise solutions as interruptions of the pedal or a pedal vibrato.

The *sfz* in **bar 196** of the violin is probably to be understood – corresponding to marking on the piano part – as a maintained *f*, so that the *p sub.* in **bar 197** (not present in the first edition) gets its justification in consideration of the *cresc.* in **bar 200**.

The rhythmic distribution of **bar 196** between violin and piano still remains somewhat doubtful, and also is interpreted very differently. The reason is probably that the original edition has separate violin and piano parts and no full score, from which would be clearer which graphic representation Beethoven would have preferred. In many earlier editions (Joachim's among them) it is represented as follows :

157
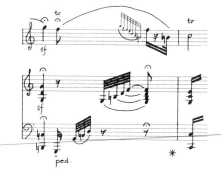

which is certainly wrong, for if the piano has a *fermata* on the last eighth-note a corresponding *fermata* would be necessary in each case for the violin, too. The violin *fermata*, however, is on the third eighth-note; thus the descending scale of the violin does not begin until the piano has already reached the last eighth-note. Hence I regard it thus:

158
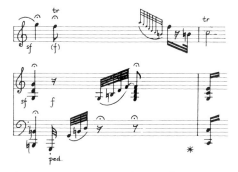

The pianist should try to begin **bar 197** right away with the initial tempo of this second movement (the theme). The piano need not go along with the *cresc.* of the violin in **bars 200–201** and could behave as the violinist did in Variation I, i.e., with accompanying figure *sempre piano*.

The theme in **bars 202–205** which is divided between the two instruments can be perfectly realized only with difficulty, as the heterogeneity of the instruments is more of a problem for us here than usual. In order to approach more closely to the desired goal I propose that the violinist prolong the first D in **bar 203** simultaneously with a *dim.* and imitate the preceding bars of the piano's *quasi staccato* but not until the continuation from the second note of the triplet. The pianist could start the last triplet of **bar 202** with a small *cresc.* and prolong the first note in **bar 204**, like the violinist in **bar 203**.

Very many violin students do not realize when they first study this work what happens rhythmicly in the piano in **bars 205**, **207**, **209** and **211**, for here there are four thirty-second-notes in the left hand, and only then do the triplets follow. Unawareness of this fact regularly leads to chaos in the ensemble.

The dynamic in the piano part missing in the first edition – that means the *pp* in **bars 214** and **220**, which is correctly supplied in most later editions – is based on the original notation of the violin part in **bar 214**. This omission is, I think, due to simple carelessness.

At the end of **bars 203–204** and **223–224** in each case there is a thirty-second-note either in the piano or in the violin, and one should take care not to play it until after the third note of the last triplet. Some pianists tend to put the *fermata*, which is not intended until the second quarter-note (G sharp) of **bar 227**, already on the trilled G at the beginning of the bar. It is also advisable not to strike the first note (A) of **bar 228** too quietly despite the *p sub.*, as otherwise the main thematic material of the right hand is overshadowed by the left, and also by the violin. The left hand in the piano should be discreet in this bar, as should the violinist.

The 'farewell phrase' in **bars 230–232**

 159

occurs four times between piano and violin and with the last playing concludes the movement. I therefore use a tiny *rit.* at the end of **bar 232** to suggest in this manner a kind of sense of finality, for the last three bars represent for me an epilogue.

The dynamic in the last but one bar is often neglected; the violinist in the first half of the bar has a *cresc.*, and the piano must come in, in the second half, with the dynamic level that the violinist has just reached. In the concluding *dim.* the partners should also match each other exactly.

Third Movement: *Presto*

This movement was, as I mentioned when discussing the last movement of the Sonata, Op. 30, No. 1, not originally intended for the *Kreutzer* but for the other A major Sonata, Op. 30, No. 1. This exchange has proved a most happy one. The thematic material in this *Presto* is mostly more violinistic and easier to play on a stringed instrument than on the piano. The maintaining of really short *staccato* notes forces on the pianist a certain restriction of speed. The tempo of this *Presto* should therefore be only as fast as the pianist manages to maintain genuine *staccato* notes. The violinist is recommended not to enter too early at the beginning of this movement, i.e., not until after the fading away of the *ff* chord of the piano. If the violinist begins really *p* before the piano chord has died away, one would not hear his entry at all.

In **bars 1–10** the violinist has the leading voice, which is then taken over by the piano, so that the string player in **bars 11–14** plays second fiddle, so to speak. This requires a dynamic differentiation, although in both cases a *p* is prescribed.

From the third eighth-note of **bar 14** onwards, the violin again plays an important role, which is taken over by the left hand of the piano in **bar 18**.

The *cresc.* added in most editions in **bars 50–51** is not to be found in the first edition but seems justified by a comparison with **bars 327–328**. **Bars 58–61** often present difficulties for the violinist, for Beethoven's way of writing is here more in accordance with pianistic usage to avoid octaves on the eighth-notes. The extra motion involved in the violinist's string-crossing to the A string for the octave is, strictly speaking, unnecessary if little bow is used for the eighth-notes and if he remains on the E string only in his imagination but plays the *sfz* very strongly and with a lot of bow. Of course, on the eighth-notes the bow should be already as close as possible to the A string which, however, must be avoided by a hair's breadth.

During the secondary theme, which starts with **bar 62**, the prescribed *p* should of course be observed, but one might consider playing **bars 70–77** in *pp*. Although this idea does not correspond to the Urtext, it does not lack a certain appeal! If the violinist opts for such a nuance, the pianist would have to act similarly in **bars 86–93**; one would have to proceed in exactly the same way, then, in **bars 339–370**.

The accompanying figures which, in **bars 62–93** and **339–370**, occur in turn in the piano and the violin are always concluded after the first eighth-note of the bar; in the piano this holds true for **bars 62**, **69–70** and **77** as well as **339**, **346–347** and **354**, and in the violin for **bars 77**, **85** and **93** as well as **354**, **362** and **370**. This can be clarified in, for instance, the following way:

160

From **bar 94** one must again pay attention to which of the two partners has the main voice and which the subsidiary one; for instance, the right hand of the piano dominates in **bars 94–95**, but the violin takes over the main voice from **bar 96**. The same applies for the parallel passage from **bar 371**. Although the *p sub.* in **bars 100** and **377** is very hard to realize for both instruments, it seems meaningful and worth the effort, rather than choosing the simple way of letting the *p* enter only at the second eighth-note.

The *f* in **bars 126** and **403** gives rise to various interpretations; although logically an *f* after the *ff* would be a decrease in volume, I am of the belief that we are dealing here with two chords which are emphatically stressed, even rather strengthened. The comparison with the parallel passages of **bars 399–403** does not get us any further, for in the original edition in the piano the *ff* is entirely missing, and in the violin only an *f* is written instead of the original *ff*; but in **bar 403** we find again in both parts the enigmatic *f*. A step towards the resolution of this problem is brought about by the notation *f* in **bars 134** and **411** in the piano which clearly accentuates these chords with special stress. In comparison to **bar 148**, where it is written, the *appoggiatura* of the piano in **bar 425** is missing, and it is at least questionable whether here one should stick to the letter of the text or not.

Just as questionable is the dynamic notation at **bar 152**, where the *p* in the piano is already present at the beginning of the bar, but in the violin part of the first edition not until the third eighth-note. In the parallel passage, **bar 429**, the *p* in the violin is also written on the third eighth-note, but this time in the piano not until the next bar. In this case I find it far more convincing to use the dynamic prescribed for **bars 429–430** in **bars 152–153** as well. The fact in itself that the *p* in **bars 152–153** in the piano is written twice allows the conclusion that the first *p* should have been deleted but was overlooked.

The entry of the violin in **bars 177** and **454** is often made uncertain by the pianist playing the preceding scale not strictly in time.

The *cresc.* in **bar 178** does not reach its peak until the *ff* in **bar 182**, and not already at the first *sfz* in **bar 180**, as one often hears. The same goes for **bars 455–459**.

In the first edition in the violin part an *fp* is written at the beginning of **bar 194**; in the piano part, however, there is no dynamic notation at all. This raises the question of whether one wants to adjust the dynamic in **bar 202** to that of **bar 194**, or even the other way round. In this case I favour an adaptation and would play *fp* in both instruments in **bars 194** and **202**.

From **bar 206** for eight bars a notable calming down occurs in this otherwise tempestuous movement, an important and welcome interruption. A tiny slowing down of the tempo at this place does not seem sacrilegious to me!

The slurs in the violin part in **bars 207–213** are a typically pianistic notation which sometimes puzzles the violinist. It goes without saying that the first eighth-note of every bar is separated from the following quarter-note, in the same way as the pianist strikes the quarter-note a second time. In spite of the notation in 161 one should use the following bowing:

This passage proves once again that phrasing slurs and bowing slurs are not identical.

From the second half of **bar 214** to the first half of **bar 222** the piano has the main voice, and the opposite relationship starts with **bar 222**. It is advisable to observe some discretion in each case in the secondary voice. The *sfz*s which are written from **bar 239** in the piano and in the violin in turn are in this case not to be equated with an *f*, so one should always return to the *p*. Not until **bar 245** is there a *cresc.* towards a real *f*.

A difference (for me, clearly intentional) in the length with which the repeated note E in **bars 267–286** is to be held is mostly overlooked. In the violin the four E's in **bars 267–270** are without dots; they are therefore to be played longer than in the following bars (which have shortening dots). The same process is repeated in **bars 275–283**. The repeated E's in the piano are short, with the exception of those which are written as octaves in the left hand. The three bass notes E in **bars 284–286** are to be held as full quarter-notes, but must be different from the following four bars (E sharp) which have a pedal. The end of **bar 290** is often played with rhythmic imprecision, because, while the pianist quite rightly holds the *rit.* to the last eighth-note, the violinist already takes this sixth eighth-note wrongly *a tempo*, which never results in a really impeccable ensemble.

I use the *p* which is written in the second half of **bar 303** also in **bar 295**.

As regards the violin figure in **bars 335–338**, I refer the reader to my remarks on **bars 58–61** (p. 157) except that the string-crossing is here employed in the opposite way – from the lower string to the upper. In the original there is an O (i.e., open string) over the quarter-note E, and one does well to double these *sfz* notes:

162

In contrast to the parallel passage in the first part, this time one remains on the A string in the imagination only.

In the subsidiary theme beginning with **bar 339** one can proceed, in dynamic and phrasing, similarly to **bars 62–95**. I would remind the players to supply in both parts the *ff* missing in **bar 399**; and the pianist should consider the question of an *appoggiatura* in **bar 425**. Here also it depends on the approach: should one believe the first edition (the manuscript is lost), or could this be a printing error?

From **bar 467** the piano has without a doubt the leading upper voice, up to the thematic entry of the violin in **bar 471**:

163

From **bar 475** the piano again takes the lead up to **bar 482**, especially in the left hand of **bars 479–482**. The violinist should beware not to take the preceding *p* in the four **bars 471–474** too literally; this applies also to **bars 483–486**. The *ritardando* in **bar 486** (which unfortunately has become customary) I consider inappropriate, for in the first place any suggestion of it is missing, and in the second place – much more important – a virtually breathless striving towards the *sfz* in **bar 487** is considerably more convincing. One runs, as it were, blindly into a wall, which has a much more dramatic effect.

The following *Adagio*s (**bars 489–492** and **497–501**) are, in my opinion, often played too fast. After all, there is an essential difference between *Presto* and *Adagio* – and Beethoven did not write *Allegretto* or *Andante*!

At this place, too, true appreciation of the main and

subsidiary voices is often missing. I will try to give here a
graphic representation by writing larger and smaller notes:

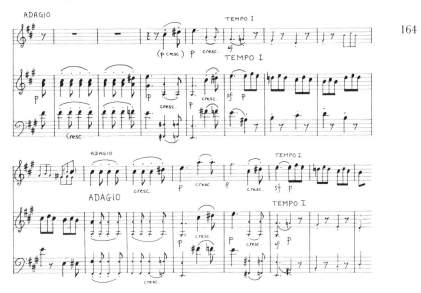

164

In the first edition in the violin part in **bar 496** we find

165

as I have shown in my music example by printing the stems
upwards, in contrast to most editions, with the exception of
Henle, where the last three eighth-notes are indicated thus:

166

If an unknown violinist plays these notes, now 'corrected', he
will surely be torn to pieces by the critics – if they notice!

For both instruments the *sfz*s in **bars 517–518** and **521**
stand for *f* up to the *p sub.* in **bar 525**. However, this no longer
applies for **bars 527**, **531**, **533** and **535**, for in **bar 535** a
special *cresc.* is asked for which leads to the triumphant *ff* at
the end of the work.

Sonata No. 10 in G major, Op. 96

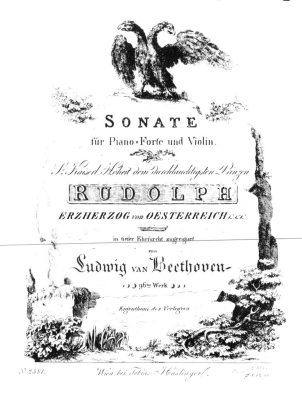

Dedicated to Prince Rudolph, Archduke of Austria

Composed probably 1812
Manuscript: Pierpont Morgan Library, New York
First Edition July 1816

Introduction

This Sonata is the last work of the series; for a stringed
instrument with piano only the two Sonatas in C major and in
D major, Op. 102, for cello and piano were still to come.

The Sonata, Op. 96, was probably written in the year 1812, at the same time as the Seventh and Eighth Symphonies, Opp. 92 and 93, and it represents a kind of turning-point in Beethoven's *œuvre*: none of the earlier Sonatas, and not even the String Quartet in F major, Op. 95, which preceded it, shows that abstract, philosophical quality which from now on characterizes all of Beethoven's output and is generally called his last period.

As we have noticed, Beethoven was but rarely prepared to make concessions for performing musicians and showed little consideration for their areas of expertise or limitation. Typical of this are the various versions of the solo part in the Violin Concerto, Op. 61, where Beethoven initially took into consideration the advice of a violinist friend; but these technically-based aids were later rejected by the composer. In the *Kreutzer* Sonata, Op. 47, one can sense, for once, a certain willingness to compromise, with the aim of exploiting to the full the virtuosity of George Bridgetower, the violinist to whom the work was originally dedicated. In this last Sonata, too, conscious concessions – even if in limited measure – were admitted, specially for the French violinist Pierre Rode. The premiere is said to have taken place on 29 December 1812 in the palace of Prince Lobkowitz, the performers being Rode and the Archduke Rudolph of Austria, Beethoven's pupil, to whom the work is dedicated. A second performance with the same interpreters followed on 7 January 1813, at a public concert.

In his *Life of Beethoven* Alexander Wheelock Thayer quotes remarks of the composer which seem to me particularly important in connection with the Tenth Sonata:[1]

> Pierre Rode, who at his peak had occupied perhaps the first place among living violinists, having been [expelled] from Russia, made a concert tour in Germany and came in December [1812] to Vienna. Spohr, whose judgement of violin playing cannot be impugned, had heard him ten years before with delight and astonishment, and now again in a public concert on January 6. He now thought that he had retrograded; he found

[1] *op. cit.*, p. 545.

Archduke Rudolph of Austria
8 January 1788–24 July 1831
Beethoven's pupil of composition and piano from 1804.
A considerable number of Beethoven's works are dedicated to the Archduke, whose role in Beethoven's life, as
patron, friend and pupil, was of the highest importance.

his playing 'cold and full of mannerisms'; he missed 'the former daring in the overcoming of difficulties', and felt himself 'particularly unsatisfied with his *cantabile* playing'. 'The public, too, seemed dissatisfied,' he says, 'at least, he could not warm it into enthusiasm.' Still, Rode had a great name; paid to and received from nobles the customary homage; and exhibited his still great talents in their salons. Beethoven must have still thought well of his powers, for he now took up and completed his Sonata, Op. 96, to be played at one of Lobkowitz's evening concerts by Rode and Archduke Rudolph.

To judge from the tone of two letters to the Archduke, for which we are indebted to Ludwig, Ritter von Köchel,[2] the composer seems to have been less satisfied with Rode's playing than he had expected. In December 1812 he wrote to the Archduke:[3]

> The copyist will be able to begin work on the last movement very early tomorrow morning. Since in the meantime I have myself been engaged on several other works, I have not hurried unduly to compose the last movement merely for the sake of being punctual, the more so as in view of Rode's playing I have had to give more thought to the composition of this movement. In our Finales we like to have fairly noisy passages, but R[ode] does not care for them – and so I have been rather hampered.

Thayer gives yet a further report about the performance of the Sonata, which appeared in a newspaper on 4 January:[4]

> The great violinist Rode recently played a new duet for Pianoforte and Violin with His Imperial Highness Archduke Rudolph at the residence of His Highness Prince Lobkowitz. It was as a whole well performed, but we must remark that the piano part was performed far more excellently, more suited to the spirit of the piece, and with more soul, than that of the violin. Mr. Rode's greatness does not seem to lie in this kind of

---

[2] Best known as the compiler of the Chronological Thematic Catalogue of Mozart's works.

[3] Translation from Anderson (ed.), *op. cit.*, Vol. 1, p. 391; see also Thayer, *op. cit.*, p. 546.

[4] *Glöggls Zeitung*, 4 January 1813, quoted in Thayer's *Life of Beethoven* only in the edition by Hermann Deiters, Breitkopf & Härtel, Leipzig, 1901, p. 351.

Jacques Pierre Rode
16 February 1774–26 November 1830
Famous French composer and violinist. A pupil of Viotti,
he wrote 13 violin concertos, many string quartets, duos,
and so on, but his classic – and still very valuable – *24
Caprices en Forme d'Études dans les 24 Tons de la Gamme*
belong among the fundamental literature of violin
teaching, to which he himself contributed a method.

music but rather in the performance of the concerto. The composition of this new duet is by Mr. Lud. van Beethoven; nothing more can be said of this work than that it leaves behind all his other works of this kind, for it surpasses almost all of them in popularity, wit, and spirit.

In our time and at a longer distance, we cannot really share the opinion of that critic. Firstly this last Sonata, with its profound style of composition which denies itself any striving for effect, is by no means the most 'popular' one of its kind, nor is it – despite some passages of 'good spirit' – really 'witty', as the term applies to Beethoven, as in, for instance, the Scherzo of the *Spring* Sonata, Op. 24.

Furthermore, the exchange of letters between Beethoven and the Archduke about the Tenth Sonata is interesting, if only because we see from it that Rode, like many others of that time – even, indeed, into the 1920's – did not study such works really intensively but, instead, mostly performed them *prima vista* as so-called *Hausmusik*. The Archduke wrote to Beethoven:[5]

> Dear Beethoven
> The day after tomorrow, Thursday, at six o'clock in the evening, there is music again at Prince Lobkowitz's, and I am supposed to repeat the sonata there with Rhode; if your health and affairs allow it I would like to see you at my house tomorrow in order to play the sonata through.
> If Rhode maybe wants to have the violin part to go over it, let me know it, so that I can send it; and also if and when you can come to me tomorrow.
> Your friend Rudolph.

Beethoven's answer to the Archduke can be read in its entirety in Anderson and Thayer; here I will quote only this extract which is relevant for us:[6]

> . . . As to Rode, if Your Imperial Highness will only be so gracious as to send me the [violin] part by the bearer of this

---

[5] *ibid.*, pp. 351–2.
[6] In Thayer (Deiters edition only) p. 352, and in Anderson, Vol. 1, pp. 401–2 (whence this translation, from which some italicization has been omitted).

letter, then I will send it on to him immediately with a billet doux from myself. He will certainly not take it amiss that I send him the part, alas! most certainly not! Would to God there were reasons to beg his pardon for doing so; for, in that case, things would indeed be in a better state.

I shall refrain from undertaking an analysis or pointing out the merits and beauties in this Sonata, too, for there are already many important books dealing most excellently with these aspects. I may point here in particular to Joseph Szigeti's little book *The Ten Beethoven Sonatas for Piano and Violin*[7] but also to *Beethovens Violinsonaten* by Justus Hermann Wetzel[8] and to Book Two of *The Art of Violin Playing* by Carl Flesch who, in his introduction,[9] has important things to say about this work, such as:

> If among the Beethoven violin sonatas one may pick out Op. 24, Op. 30, No. 2, and Op. 47 as being those most favoured by the listener, the connoisseur regards Op. 96 as the most perfected work of the whole series. Its first movement in particular represents for me a high-point of Beethovenian creation. Its significance, however, is not on the surface, for it is hardly possible adequately to translate the spiritual depth, the impressionistically delicate colors in which it is dipped into acoustic phenomena. The composition is not 'grateful'; it offers no opportunity for the deployment of typical violin cantilene, it is the most delicate filigree work, dream-wrought mood-music, with intentionally circumscribed, on occasion merely indicated means. In short, it hastens on in advance of its time in the same degree as do certain parts of the last quartets or piano sonatas. The reproduction of this movement not only calls for two players who in their ensemble stand technically as well as tonally on the highest level, but for more: the interpreters must also be able to dream, to enthuse; the blue flower must blossom in their souls. Only he who possesses this poetic empathy will be able to transmute into perfected sound the precious pith hidden in a seemingly rude wrapping.

These are truths which remain valid despite changes of taste wrought by time. It is different with Flesch's violinistic

---

[7] pp. 34–35.
[8] Unfortunately, I know of no English translation of Wetzel's book.
[9] p. 185 (translation slightly adapted).

interpretations in the same chapter of his book. More than half a century has passed since then, and changes in taste, musicology and even in average technical ability have, to some extent, created essentially different prerequisites. As with the preceding Sonatas I shall now put down in detail my experience in interpretation and technique.

First Movement: *Allegro Moderato*

At the outset one must establish whether one should use a grace-note after the trill in the theme. I have already express-ed my opinion on this in the section dealing with ornamenta-tion (pp. 24–25) to the effect that ornamentation in late Beethoven in particular should be used only where expressly prescribed by the composer, as, for instance, in the penulti-mate bar of the Scherzo. There is room, of course, for differences of opinion here: such eminent artists as Adolf Busch and Rudolf Serkin have used grace-notes after the trills in their recordings; and Arturo Toscanini, too, believed that any trill without a grace-note seems not persuasive but empty – even naked. I believe – and not only with Beethoven – that one should not be dogmatic, but carefully weigh the case of each single trill so as to avoid a mechanically stereotyped interpretation.

Insufficient attention is paid – also right at the beginning – to the division of voices between the two instruments. In the first six bars plus upbeat the violin has the lead, after which, even up to **bar 22**, the piano does. This sequence is reversed in the recapitulation from **bar 142**. Here the piano leads in the beginning, but from **bar 148** plus upbeat the violin takes over the lead up to **bar 161**.

Here also the dynamic must be followed very faithfully. The swell which is so often heard, especially in **bars 17–19**, should be resisted and one should observe a linear melodic style. On the other hand (as everywhere in Beethoven) the *p sub*.s play an essential role, as in **bars 22**, **25**, **28** and **33**. But also the sudden *f*s in **bars 26** and **30** should not be provided, almost 'politely', with introductory *crescendi*. The dramatic and unexpected emergence of these dynamic contrasts is one of the characteristic traits of Beethoven. One should resist the easy tendency to introduce *piani* with *dim.* and *forti* with *cresc.* In **bar 19** in the violin the last eighth-note – since it is a repetition of the previous eighth-note – stands separately, i.e., no longer tied, which is not really in accordance with the sense, and is obviously only an instrumental make-shift. Not only is there a slur in the piano in the same bar up to the end of the bar (the violin has exactly the same phrasings in **bars 10–21** as the piano), the slur is also carried through to the end of the bar in the parallel passage in **bar 158** for both instruments. The repetition of E flat in the piano in this bar on the last two eighth-notes of the right hand does not present an instrumental problem, although in some older editions the last eighth-note is wrongly written as D. Both manuscript and first edition unmistakably give E flat.

I would propose a solution for the place in question, **bar 19** in the violin, by carrying through the slur up to the end of the bar, but changing fingers on the last eighth-note:

167

The same technique is valid for the violin in **bar 80**, for the last two notes must be articulated twice despite the *legato* slur. The Henle edition questions whether the first chord in **bar 21**, which is written in manuscript and first edition, is actually a slip of the pen, and for this reason the G in the right hand is omitted there. The same point of view is also held by other editors; Joseph Joachim, for instance, was one. For me the original notation is completely justifiable:

168

Neither partner should yield to the generally observed tendency to *cresc.* in the third bar of the secondary theme, nor to an *sfz* in the fourth bar – in the piano **bars 43–44** and the violin in **bars 51–52**. My advice is always to execute the accompanying figure in the violin in **bars 41–47** on two different strings, as is also evident from the final double-stopped note:

169

In this case the idea is easy to translate, whereas in the parallel passage in the recapitulation other difficulties arise. In **bars 182–183** I have often heard – even in the concert hall – the repeated E simply played on a single string, whereas the first note of every triplet, as a bass note, should always be played on a lower string. So in **bars 182–183** the first E of every triplet should be on the G string:

170

The varied designation of the note-values in the left hand of the piano in **bars 49–54** and **188–193** is obviously significant and deliberate; I mention it merely because it is overlooked all too often.

From **bar 59** the difference in the nature of the two instruments poses the usual problems with the dynamic. An ideal combination of the double stops in the violin with the sound of the left hand of the piano is very difficult to achieve. Normally in the piano every one of these chords is necessarily a *dim.* while most of the time the violinist maintains his double stops in the same degree of loudness. An adaptation by the violinist should in such cases be a matter of musical course, e.g., an unwritten tiny *dim.* in every bar. Unfortunately many violinists do not know the work well enough, having neglected to familiarize themselves with the piano part. It has always been surprising, and, to me, incomprehensible, how pianists (some quite eminent ones among them) completely ignore the rhythmically precise way Beethoven wrote down the chain of trills in the right hand in **bars 63–71** as in the parallel passage in **bars 202–210** and, in particular, how they disregard the *sfz*s on every quarter-note in **bars 68–70** and **207–209**. These bars are often played as a single, sustained long trill, which certainly does not correspond to Beethoven's intentions. The violin's commentary in **bar 72** up to the first eighth-note of **bar 75** must not overshadow the more important events in the piano part; on the other hand the violinist may provide a light *cresc.* on the upbeat of the second eighth-note in **bar 75** as he takes over the thematic material. In the piano, of course, it is the other way round: here the last three eighth-notes in **bar 75** should rather be in a light *dim.* A deliberate single-bar phrasing is in my opinion advisable in **bars 72–73** for the piano; the same applies for the violin in **bars 76–77**. In **bar 80** I advise (as I have mentioned before, on p. 170) changing fingers on the last two notes of the violin part so as to keep to the original phrasing:

171

For both instruments in **bar 91**, there is the danger of playing the *p sub.* all too quietly, without considering that there is still a *dim.* to follow, which leads to the *pp* in **bar 94**. The same applies to the *p* in **bar 98**, and likewise to **bar 105** for the piano and **bar 106** for the violin. At the end of **bar 115** I recommend a slight hesitation to introduce the very special and abstract atmosphere from **bar 116**. It is a matter of individual taste whether the violinist executes the two *pizz.* in **bars 139–140** with the left or the right hand. For sound, correct dynamic gradation and natural movement, I have always preferred to play the *pizz.* with the right hand, and in such a way that the plucking movement corresponds, as it were, to a downbow, and the following trill finds a natural continuation in the upbow.

The layout of the recapitulation, which begins in **bar 141**, is exactly opposite to that of the exposition at the beginning of the movement. This time the piano begins (see also my remarks on p. 169). Accordingly it is clear that the violin (in contrast to the exposition) takes over the leading part in **bars 150–161** also. Shortly before this the pianist should execute the surprising and inspired modulation on the last quarter-note of **bar 148** with a slight hesitation, gently and tenderly.

In **bar 158** problems arise again in the violin part: the penultimate eighth-note has no accidental either in the manuscript or in the first edition, and could therefore be an A. The German journal *Die Musikforschung*[10] recommends an A flat, as do some modern editions. This is entirely possible; we could be dealing with an omission in manuscript and first edition, but I think one should consider whether an A is not equally appropriate!

I have already pointed to the last two eighth-notes of the right hand in the piano in **bar 158**. The repetition of the E flat matches the violin part in **bar 19** and should not, as in some editions, be changed to D. (Incidentally, both manuscript and first edition show two E flats.)

The *p sub.* in **bars 161**, **164**, **167** and **172** should be taken just as seriously as in the beginning in **bars 25–33**, and therefore not, as so often happens, with transitions from *cresc.* to *f* and *dim.* to *p*. As regards the triplet accompanying figure in the violin in **bars 180–185**, I refer to my remarks on page 171.

In the secondary theme in **bars 180–194** the different octave transitions in the piano and the violin are interesting. In the exposition each instrument in its third bar plays exactly the same downward octave leaps. I suppose that Beethoven thought it too risky to send the violinists into the 'regions of eternal snows'; thus the beginning of **bars 188–189** is already an octave lower than the piano, but this is true also of **bars 192–193**. It looks very much like a compromise when (as written) the first triplet in **bar 194** prescribes an upward jump of a seventh. The avoidance of the high positions seems all the more remarkable as Beethoven had no scruples in this respect either in the Violin Concerto or in the *Romances*. It is perhaps due to the fact that the Sonatas were written more for

---

[10] Vol. 5, 1952, pp. 53–54.

'domestic use', not practised but played more or less *prima vista* – as is shown in Beethoven's complaint about Rode's performance. The reason may also have been a certain mistrust of Rode's technical abilities. Today there is no particular difficulty, even for the average violinist, in playing the theme in the way it was written for the piano. This brings us to a general matter of conscience: there are quite a lot of places where Beethoven prescribes octave leaps downwards because the pianos of his day (although this applies also to other instruments – flutes, for example) did not have the range of modern instruments. We must decide whether we are to follow Beethoven's text exactly, despite the instrumental limitations he had to contend with, or to avoid making the octave leaps – an extremely difficult decision!

For **bars 198–201** I refer the violinist to my remarks on **bars 59–62**, and for the pianist comparing the trills in **bars 202–210** to **bars 63–71**. The dynamic in **bar 214** in both instruments is exactly as in **bar 75**!

The violinist should proceed in **bar 219** as in **bar 80**, only a fifth lower. In **bars 223–233** the dynamic is to be carried out just as carefully as in **bars 84–94**. I should like to draw the pianist's attention to the fact that the coda starts with a trill in **bar 238**, maintaining the corresponding phrasing. In both instruments the trills should always be without grace-notes. The dynamic in **bar 260**, especially in the piano, should be strictly observed, for the sixteenth-note passage really starts only with the second sixteenth-note; the same is true for the violin in **bar 262**. For this reason the violin plays the four sixteenth-notes in **bar 261**, as well as the first note of the next bar, as a subordinate voice, and from the second sixteenth-note of **bar 262** steps into the foreground as the soloist. Also the left hand of the piano enters in **bar 264** only after the beat.

The slurs in the violin part in **bars 262–263** written in the first edition seem sensible to me, although in the manuscript the slur is over a full five quarter-notes:

upper slur, first edition

lower slur, manuscript

The fingering in the penultimate quarter-note appears in the manuscript and the first edition, so it must originate from Beethoven himself. To clarify the matter, the piano can take the leading voice with the last quarter-note in **bar 275** but must retreat in favour of the violin on the last quarter-note of the next bar, then to resume the main voice in the next bar with the last quarter-note, up to the ending.

The slurs in each bar in the two instruments in **bars 268–273** are according to the original and should not at all be changed, as they have been in some editions.

Second Movement: *Adagio Espressivo*

This movement, one of the most profound, most heartfelt and most sublime, is among the most beautiful compositions in all music. Perhaps only in the slow movement of the Sonata, Op. 30, No. 1, and in Mozart's great B flat major Sonata, K.454, can one find again a comparably ideal dialogue of these two instruments.

At the outset, in **bar 3** in the bass the lower octave E is missing; it has been added in modern editions in parentheses. Here again we encounter the dilemma of the transpositions of octaves and whether to remain faithful to the text or to supplement it in a meaningful fashion.[11] The missing E in the bass was simply not available on the piano of that time.

Many (even Urtext) editions give no dynamic indication for the beginning of this movement in the piano, but in the manuscript as in the first edition a *p* is quite clearly written.

In this first piano theme of eight bars I see the last sixteenth-note in **bar 4** almost as an upbeat to the continuation of the remaining four bars. This necessitates a similar dynamic decrease on the first three eighth-notes of this bar, e.g., in **bar 8** where the theme ends with the fifth sixteenth-note. It is therefore for the pianist to play the last three sixteenth-notes of **bar 8** as accompaniment, just as the violin has to after the first three notes of **bar 9**. This sequence of

---

[11] See my remarks on the first movement on p. 173–174.

notes is a repetition of the closing of the theme which was played by the piano one bar earlier:

173

Despite the *sotto voce* the violin should play this warmly and tenderly and only then start the accompaniment.

The original phrasing slurs of Beethoven in this movement confirm my repeated observation – in other connections as well – that phrasing slurs are not identical to bowings and bowing slurs. While I try to realize all of a composer's phrasings without qualification, bow changes are often unavoidable. Therefore, especially today, it is of particular importance that the violinist effect an inaudible bow change. With such bow control, the composer's phrasing can be realized despite some bow changes. To give one example: I consider it impossible to carry out Beethoven's phrasing in this movement (**bars 26–31**) with exact observance of the desired dynamic in a single violin bowing slur. Something similar can be found in the slow movement of the Second *Rasumovsky* Quartet, Op. 59, No. 2, where there is also a phrasing which is not feasible as a slur for the violin.

Much could be said about the original pedalling in the piano part – especially in this movement – but I prefer to leave that to more competent people (such as Günter Ludwig in his Postscript to this book). There are some incomprehensible instructions here which probably have to be interpreted differently on the modern grand piano than they would have been on an instrument of Beethoven's day. The comparatively short *cresc.*s in **bars 21–22** and **23–24** can have a steeper and faster development in both instruments than, for instance, **bars 25–29** whose *cresc.*s extend over a whole five bars rather than over one-and-a-half.

The cadence-like **bars 32–35** of the violin can be shaped freely without étude-like metronomic adherence. The *p sub.* in **bar 38** in the violin part is characterized by the instruction *mezza voce*, and in the piano is indicated by *p*. The expression instruction *semplice*, missing at the beginning of the movement in the piano, suggests an introspective inner warmth, which because of this very simplicity is not easy to realize. The phrasing recommended for the piano applies also for the violin, so that in **bar 41** the last sixteenth-note is delayed as if it were an upbeat. In **bar 45** the last three sixteenth-notes of the violin must again be played as an accompaniment, i.e., falling off dynamically. Although the main interest, from **bar 49** to the beginning of **bar 54**, lies in the piano, the violin should not interpret its part purely as accompaniment but as a tonally beautiful, expressive commentary. The sudden and solitary double stop in the violin in **bar 54** may seem strange to the unthinking student. Of course, the lower G is the last note of the preceding phrase while the top E flat announces the beginning of the leading violin part. I would provide the lower note with a *dim.* and the top one with a *cresc.*, which, technically, is not easy to execute.

An unusual notation is the *p* in **bar 58**, written not on the *appoggiatura* but on the main note, E flat. It is, I think, entirely plausible to regard this *appoggiatura* as the completion of the preceding phrase of the *cresc.* which leads to the G, and to delay the entry of the *p sub.* until the main note, E flat. Certainly the piano should in this case enter with the right hand on the main note of the violin.

In **bar 61** in the violin part there is in fact a *p sub.* on the last eighth-note, but the *p* written in the piano part in many editions (even in different places) we do not find at all in the first edition. The customary solution, letting the piano play *cresc.* by a whole sixteenth-note longer than the violin, is by no means convincing. In my opinion piano and violin should either start the *p* at the same time, on the last eighth-note, or not until the beginning of the next bar, as is written in the piano part of the first edition.

The pedalling in **bar 65** brings additional problems for the violinist. The rhythmic notation is the same for the violin as for the piano – except that the violin is not equipped with a pedal. I believe long notes with slight separations to be suitable for both instruments, especially because the last pedal notation in **bar 65** does not have a cancellation mark; I thus tend to the view not to sustain the pedal over three bars.

Third Movement: *Scherzo. Allegro*

This movement is usually regarded as being 'playful', a view I do not share at all, despite the marking 'Scherzo'. Its mode of expression – with the exception of the Trio – is rather uncanny, shadowy, tense, even alarming or, to quote Beethoven himself (although in another connection[12]) *beklemmt* – a word that can hardly be translated into other languages; one can paraphrase its meaning to some extent by a multitude of other words, but to render its true content with a single word is practically impossible.* All eighth-notes are, without exception, written without shortening dots. I am thus firmly convinced that they should be played to their full value by both instruments – neither *staccato* for the piano nor *martelé* or *spiccato* for the violin. Furthermore, the *sfp* on every upbeat underlines the uncanny nature of the movement. The violinist will find it best to arrange his bowing in the following manner:

It need hardly be mentioned that the theme of the first eight bars lies in the piano part and that the following eight bars in the violin are no more than a faithful repetition. This situation is repeated in the second half of the theme, with the piano in **bars 17–24** and violin in **bars 25–32**. But I stress it here because violinists often tend to take over the leading role, even while the piano carries the theme, instead of fulfilling the function of a harmonic accompaniment, together with the left hand of the piano.

As I have said, the character of the Trio is quite different from that of the Scherzo; here a certain Viennese placidity,

---

[12] See p. 117.

* The nearest English equivalent would probably be 'uneasy', 'anxious' or 'oppressed'. –TRANSL.

even *Gemütlichkeit*, becomes noticeable. The tempo in the Trio can, in my opinion, be a little slower than in the Scherzo. At the beginning, in the first eight bars, **33—40**, the violin leads and in **bars 41—48** is faithfully echoed by the piano.

The four bars in the violin, **49—52**, which are then interpolated are conspicuously Viennese and could have originated with the Waltz King, Johann Strauss, or perhaps with Fritz Kreisler. From **bar 53** the violin begins the canon which is taken over by the piano in **bar 57**. Here we encounter the difficulty of following the composer's wishes on dynamics, for the *cresc.*, which reaches its climax with the third quarter-note of **bar 64**, and the subsequent *dim.* are spread over a considerably long stretch: *cresc.* over all of twelve bars, and *dim.* over as many as fifteen. A carefully graded, slow development in both directions is thus necessary. The coda-like last eight bars of this Trio should be like a whisper, with the utmost delicacy. A tiny concluding *calando* right at the end seems appropriate to me. It is noteworthy that Beethoven wrote violin fingerings quite sporadically, as in **bars 37**, **55** and **58** which he obviously considered to be complicated. One should be firmly advised against their use: they are clumsy and primitive!

In the real coda, where the theme of the Scherzo lies again in the piano in the first eight bars, followed by the violin up to the end of the movement, it appears for the first time in a calming, conciliatory and peaceful major. I thus take the coda in a tempo only slightly slower than the Scherzo, rather closer to the tempo of the Trio. At the end, the trill in the violin is originally marked with a grace-note and is, for me, further proof that in his later compositions Beethoven specified the ornamentation he wished much more exactly (see my remarks on grace-notes at the beginning of this chapter – p. 169). It was Beethoven's express wish that the *da capo* of the Scherzo be printed out again in its entirety, a request observed in the first edition and, largely, in later ones.

Fourth Movement: *Poco Allegretto*

This movement begins with a jovial theme which, according to various reliable sources, was a well-known Viennese popular song of Beethoven's time[13] – an explanation that seems entirely acceptable when one considers how often Beethoven took up commonplace themes, as well as those of other composers, and developed them in grand and profound variations (I am thinking here of, for instance, the *Kakadu* Variations, Op. 121a, the *Diabelli* Variations, Op. 120, and also the Variations for piano trio, Op. 44). And in this movement, too, we have a theme and variations, so that a comparison forces itself on us, so to speak.

The articulation in the theme should be followed with careful precision, especially by the pianists, for in my experience they often play the phrasing wrongly, like this:

175

instead of:

176

which would not happen so easily to violinists if they followed the original bowings. The slurs in the first edition, which differ from most later editions (and the manuscript), seem to me of some importance. First, in the original edition, **bar 7** in the violin part is slurred to the first eighth-note of the following bar:

177

In the right-hand of the piano **bar 8** is slurred to the first quarter-note of the next bar:

[13] Gustav Nottebohm (in *Beethoveniana: Aufsätze und Mittheilungen*, J. Rieter-Biedermann, Leipzig, 1872) draws attention to a similar theme in a singspiel by J.A. Hiller, *Der Teufel ist los*, which was very popular at this time.

In **bar 13** in many editions there is a slur for both instruments from the first quarter-note to the following two sixteenth-notes:

In the original edition the following is written:

which to me seems much more appropriate.

In the first edition a slur is given in the violin part in **bar 22** up to and including the first eighth-note of **bar 24**:

Here the slur in the manuscript seems preferable:

The tempo of this theme should not be too fast, both because of its Viennese *gemütlich* character and because of the marking *Poco Allegretto*, that is, approaching *andantino*. Incidentally, in the violin part of the original edition there is the heading *Poco allegretto Variazioni*, which, as far as I know, is not recorded in any subsequent edition. There are many adherents to the theory that one should take all variations, always and everywhere, in the same rigid tempo. I heartily disagree with this view, first, because Beethoven himself was a *rubato* player *par excellence*; secondly, because it is part of the interpretative task of the performer to give each variation its appropriate expression, which often requires agogic differentiation; and finally, because in extreme cases tempo changes are prescribed by the composer himself, such as, in this movement, the *adagio espressivo* at **bar 145** and the *allegro* at the end of **bar 173**, with, at the conclusion, even *poco adagio* at the end of **bar 275** and *presto* at **bar 288**.

In the first variation, **bars 32–48**, varying and sometimes illogical slurs are noted in the first edition, so that I share the opinion of some editors who do not consider a little more 'order' here sacrilegious.

In the second variation, **bars 48–80**, both instrumentalists should not overlook the rhythmic difference of the first note of every bar: except for the last bar, the left hand of the piano always has a quarter-note; so does the right hand in **bars 57–63** and **72–79**. The violinist also should be careful to sustain fully the quarter-note in the accompanying figures in **bars 49–55** and **64–71** so as to bring out the intended contrast to the eighth-note in the thematic material. Violinists may find it of interest that I always play the phrase with a mordent on the G string and so make clear the two voices through the difference in sound of the strings (**bars 56–64**):

183

The same applies to **bars 72–80**:

184

There are simpler and safer fingerings, of course, but then violin playing is easier in any case if one does not make higher musical demands! In the third variation, **bars 81–112**, the upper and lower voices alternate every eight bars; the piano has the upper voice first, in **bars 81–88**; the violin takes over the lead from the last eighth-note of **bar 88** and repeats exactly what the piano has played previously. With the upbeat of the last eighth-note in **bar 96** the piano takes over the upper voice again, and the violin with the upbeat to **bar 104**. Very curious is the oddity (if not an oversight) that the violin repeats exactly the previous statement of the piano in **bars 89–96** and **104–112**, with the oddly single difference that in **bar 106** the second eighth-note of the violin part is written as B and in the piano, at exactly the same spot (**bar 98**) as F sharp, possibly to avoid the doubling of the F sharp, since the piano here varies the accompanying figure.

The *espressivo* which some editions add in the violin part in **bar 97** is better removed, for according to the letter (*espressivo* only in the piano part) as well as the spirit of the music the violin here has only the lower voice. It would be different if in the violin part in **bar 105** the editor had added an *espressivo* in brackets, for here the violin takes over the parallel passage of the piano (**bar 97**) which had been marked *espressivo* by the composer.

The *a tempo* in the piano part in **bar 101** (in the violin part this notation is missing in manuscript and original edition, but is correctly supplied by most later editions) gives rise to the most divergent interpretations. To be sure, this *a tempo* would make no sense without a preceding tempo change – not an *accelerando*, which is quite unthinkable; which leaves only the *un poco ritenuto* added in some editions. The question of dynamics turns out to be somewhat more difficult, because in **bar 97** in the piano part only a *cresc.* is written and it is softened immediately afterward by a *dim.* This *cresc.* extends over no less than sixteen bars to the *f* in **bar 113**. That the violin watches or rather listens to this unconcernedly is unlikely, so that in **bar 97** instead of the *espressivo* usually added a *cresc.* ⪫ , similarly bracketed, should be written. It is strange, if understandable, that many interpreters supply a background to tempo changes through an unintentional and uncontrolled dynamic. Thus if a change of tempo takes place before the *a tempo* in **bar 101**, it is almost always played with the *cresc.* intended; but in the *a tempo* a *p sub.* is often inserted, which is not really justified.

In the next variation, **bars 113–144**, one should again observe exactly which of the partners has the upper voice, so as to clarify the actual relationship to the audience here, too. In **bars 115–116** the piano dominates alone while the violin rests, unlike **bars 119–120**, where the violin has the upper voice, as again in **bars 123–124**. In **bars 127–128** it is the turn of the piano again, as, obviously, also in **bars 131–132**. In **bars 136–135** and **139–140** the violin leads again, but at the end of the variation, in **bars 143–144**, the piano has the main voice. This relationship is appropriately carried over into the next variation, where the piano is accompanied by the violin. Before I turn to this next, *Adagio*, variation I should like to point out that quite often – even in public concerts – both performers fail to concentrate sufficiently here: the chords in the two parts differ rhythmicly, and without attention the chords in the two parts can mistakenly sound simultaneously!

And now to the *Adagio* variation: the eighth-notes of the violin should be adjusted in sound, dynamics and length to the left hand of the piano in a truly chamber-music spirit; every note should thus be given a very light accent at the beginning, and, because of the nature of the piano, a tiny *dim.* should be used on every eighth-note. I would make a plea for all the trills in this variation to be played without grace-notes, although the temptation is very strong, particularly in the first bar of the piano and in **bar 149** of the violin. 'You shall renounce, renounce,' as the saying has it!*

Many pianists and violinists sustain the eighth-note in **bar 148**, which has a *fermata*, throughout the descending chromatic cadenza of the piano. This makes no sense at all to me, first, as no pedalling is prescribed, and, secondly, as this fourth eighth-note is written in the same way in the violin part as for both hands in the piano. In my opinion, the violin and the left hand of the piano should stop at the same point before the beginning of the cadenza so as to avoid harmonic chaos. The same is true also for the second piano cadenza. The marking *langsam* (slow), written in the first edition at the first

---

* The German original is a well-known line from Goethe's *Faust*, Part I: 'Entbehren sollst du, sollst entbehren'. – TRANSL.

piano cadenza (at the second it is missing, presumably because it goes without saying), is not always observed by pianists. Certainly it should be shaped freely – as *rubato* – but with a quiet and slow basic mood. It should not be forgotten, after all, that these cadenzas are in an *adagio* variation.

Between the last note, F sharp, of the piano part at the first instance and later B (in **bar 156**) the violin takes over at exactly the same pitch, so that in his intonation the violinist has to conform exactly to the piano. After a brief dying-away of the piano sound, which is not followed by a rest, the violinist can rise gradually to the playing of the theme. In **bar 152** the last two eighth-notes for the violin are to be understood as a subsidiary voice.

The long sustained F sharp in the violin in **bars 153–156** cannot be well realized tonally in this slow tempo without bow changes. I use a trick which I am happy to disclose here: I change the bow whenever the piano strikes exactly the same note in the right hand – in **bars 154–155**, for instance, on the third eighth-note. This provides good camouflage and the long F sharp really sounds like *one* sustained note. In **bar 158** the violinists will find it advisable to play the last C also on the A string, so as to be able to execute a genuine *legato* between the first two eighth-notes of the next bar without having to cross onto two non-adjacent strings. In **bars 160–162** the first eighth-note of the violin should still be played *espressivo*, and as an accompaniment only from the second eighth-note on. **Bar 163** may be freely shaped by the violinist, a liberty with which the pianist can comply sympathetically. At the end of **bar 163** in the first edition of the violin part (not in the piano) there is a *rit.* but in **bar 164** the *p* and *dolce* are only in the piano part. These markings are obviously valid for both instruments. The *p* after the *cresc.* in **bar 170** is missing in both parts of the first edition but is present in the manuscript.

In **bar 176** of the *Allegro* the sixth sixteenth-note in the right hand of the piano is undoubtedly an error, for this leap of a third does not occur in **bars 174** and **178** nor in the violin part in **bars 182** and **184** where the note sequence is of the same kind. It should therefore be corrected as follows:

185

One should refrain from the customary *sfz* in **bars 181, 189** and **197**. An *sfz* in **bar 204** is missing in the first edition but probably should be there.

It remains a moot point whether the second eighth-note in **bar 218** should be a G or, in accordance with the sequence of the *fugato*, a G sharp. In **bars 222, 226**, and **230** the descending second eighth-note is really a semitone while in **bar 234** for once a whole tone is written. My personal view is that the second eighth-note in **bar 218** is intended as G, although the same note sequence in **bar 226** of the violin part shows a G sharp.

The last two eighth-notes in **bar 223** are, in the manuscript and first edition, twice written as B flat, the justification for which is highly doubtful, as, to remain in keeping with other musical lines, the last note would have to be an A. Manuscript

186   and first edition: or: 187

Neither interpreter should forget that the repetition of the beginning of this movement, in **bar 245**, is already within the *allegro* marked from **bar 174**, that is, considerably faster than at the beginning which is *poco allegretto*.

In **bars 261–264** the violin has the upper voice, and I recommend that the pianist exercise restraint. The situation is reversed in **bars 265–267**.

In **bars 270–271** in the violin part we find more of Beethoven's rather primitive fingerings; it is particularly important not to use them because this passage, even today, has the reputation of being risky and dangerous.[14]

The *poco adagio* should be played tenderly, as if it were a reminiscence, and the thematic division between the two instruments should be carried out in ideal tonal and dynamic unity. A gradual diminishing of the dynamic and of the expression in the last four bars before the *Presto* seems to me

[14] See Carl Flesch, *op. cit.*, Book Two, pp. 185–191.

appropriate, and an intensification through an unwritten *ff* in the last four bars is no sacrilege.

Now for a short personal coda: I most warmly recommend that all interpreters take this unique and superb Sonata, Op. 96, to their hearts, even more than the works of this series which preceded it. Beside all the other splendid Sonatas of Beethoven I hold this last in particular as the crown of the genre. My wish is that all its interpreters should attempt to discover the deeper meaning of this work; its interpretation is not easy, but a profound musical and spiritual experience will be theirs.

Postscript from the Pianist's Point of View

GÜNTER LUDWIG

Reflections on Beethoven's Pedal Notations

The use of the pedal is generally counted as one of the liberties the pianist may take, comparable to the violinist's freedom of bowing (as far as the composer allows it) and of choice of string and vibrato. It is in the pedalling that a player's individual tonal imagination shows itself most strongly. The *ped.* signs of composers are thus frequently disregarded. One uses pedal according to one's feeling, to intensify or for nuance of the sound, to support the *legato*, and so on.

In performance of piano music of the Romantic period one almost always uses the pedal. A performance without enough pedal generally sounds dry and dull. Even in Beethoven's piano music it is customary today (probably even necessary) to use plenty of pedal for the obvious reason that our contemporary instruments do not sound well without it.

Comparing the pianos of Beethoven's time with our modern instruments, we find that the latter give less resonance than the older ones, even though their volume of sound is smaller; and because of this increased volume of sound in modern pianos, the use of the pedal in sustained bass notes sometimes causes problems. There is an example of this in Violin Sonata No. 9 in A major, Op. 47, second movement, **bars 205–212**:

In the Violin Sonatas Beethoven gives *ped.* notations in Sonatas Nos. 5, 6, 7, 9 and 10. This always means the right-hand pedal, i.e., lifting and dropping of the dampers.

Joseph Haydn specifies, in his Sonata in C major, Hob. No. XVI, 150 (1795), 'open pedal', meaning the raising of the dampers to effect the vibration of all the strings:

The notation for the use of pedals developed gradually around 1800. In that year, in the manuscript of the Sonata, Op. 24, in the second movement, Beethoven wrote '*senza sordino*', by which he meant: 'with (right) pedal'. And at the beginning of the Piano Sonata in C sharp minor, Op. 27, No. 2, he writes: *Si deve suonare questo pezzo delicatissimamente e senza sordino*. In a sketch of around the year 1790 he writes: 'with the knee'

(meaning the lateral knee lever for raising the dampers). After 1800 the notation *ped.* gradually prevails. The *una corda* pedal (the 'shift' pedal) is never called for in the Violin Sonatas. But this does not mean that one may not use it.

In 1803 Beethoven received an Erard grand piano with four pedals (*una corda*, moderator, mute, and buff stop), and we can assume with certainty that he used to the full the newly-developed possibilities of sound. He also exploited fully the range of his pianos, and when, around the year 1800, he wanted to go beyond the F''' he had to make do with the lower octave. For example, in the Sonata in E flat major, Op. 12, No. 3, first movement, **bars 56−57**, the octave notes F sharp''' and G''' should of course be added:

190

Beethoven's Pedal Signs and Proposals for their Execution

Sonata No. 5 in F major, Op. 24 (*Spring* Sonata)

Ped. at the end of the second movement (resonance − full pedal):

191

Sonata No. 6 in A major, Op. 30, No. 1

Ped. at the end of the second movement (*ped.* through the rest – half pedal):

Sonata No. 7 in C minor, Op. 30, No. 2

First movement, **bars 216–217** (combining a *crescendo* passage and resonance for two *staccato* chords – full pedal):

At the end of the second movement keep the *crescendo* chord *p* and without pedal until the fourth quarter-note (*cresc.*-effect), the last chord *pp* and almost without pedal. In this way one can approximate the desired effect:

The *ped.* signs in these three Sonatas are not really worthy of note, by which I mean one would use pedal in these passages in the same way, or very similarly, if nothing were written. Speculation that Beethoven wanted pedalling only where marked is, I think, wide of the mark. In the G major Sonata, Op. 30, No. 3, for instance, there is no *ped.* sign at all – and of course one cannot play the Sonata without pedal.

To be sure, some passages which are marked by *ped.* in the Ninth and Tenth Sonatas (Opp. 47 and 96) are problematic and should be reconsidered.

Sonata No. 9 in A major, Op. 47 (*Kreutzer* Sonata)

First movement

Bars 36−37:

The *ped.* encompasses a whole *ff* passage. The release should not occur until after the rest in the next bar. The piano here can often overshadow the *p* entry of the violin. One should not play the last C in the bass too strongly and should hold the *fermata* for a long time. At the entry of the violin (fourth quarter-note) one should raise the pedal halfway, and fully at the beginning of the next bar. In this way one achieves more or less the desired effect.

Bars 115–116:

196

Start the first *adagio* bar *mp*, the second half of the bar *cresc.* with pedal, and the second bar *pp* and almost without pedal.

Bars 561–574:

197

In my opinion this *ped.* sign is written two bars too early. In this way the difference between the group with the separated quarter-notes and the group with the slurred half-notes is not brought out – and Beethoven would hardly have intended to equalize them. The pedal should not be changed in the last bars but be gradually lifted more and more in order to thin out the sound. In **bar 574** a *ritardando* is recommended, and in **bar 579** *ped.* not until the second half of the bar (*cresc.*); in **bar 580** release the pedal gradually (*dim.*).

Second movement

Variation III, **bars 113–114** and **132–133**:

198

In the first bar use half-pedal from the second sixteenth-note (*senza cresc.*), and in the second bar full *ped.* at the beginning of the bar (*cresc.*).

Bars 192–193:

199

The pedal can be used exactly as written, if one takes the *staccato* D in the bass not too strongly and the F sharp very quietly. For added security, I touch the D in the bass again, silently, after playing the chord. In this way I can – in case there is too much resonance at the end of the bar – lift the pedal halfway without losing the D in the bass and without breaking off the characteristic mixed sound (major – minor). If one holds the D in the bass with the *sostenuto* pedal (middle pedal), I do not find the effect satisfying.

The coda of the second movement contains *ped.* signs which give us a clear indication of the coloration and resonance Beethoven had in mind here. At this point the use of the pedal demands the utmost flexibility and an alert ear. In this case it is just as important to know how to manage the pedal as where to apply it.

From **bar 205** on one should play the low F in the bass *pp*, and not depress the pedal too deeply (see pp. 189–190). **Bars 214–216**:

200

Start with half pedal and during the *cresc.* gradually press the pedal down fully. At the *dim.* raise the pedal again gradually.

The rests in **bars 219–222** are difficult to make audible. It is best to treat the pedal very lightly in **bar 220** and hold it in this position. In this case we depend on the even functioning of dampers and pedal. It is self-evident that the last bars of the movement must be pedalled:

201

Third Movement

Bars 122–126:

Pedal and dynamic precisely as written.

Bars 284–290:

If the three bars before the beginning of the *ped.* sign are played without pedal, the pedal effect comes out most beautifully. The sound of the piano in **bars 287–290** is supposed to blend with the C sharp of the violin. This is best achieved with half-pedal so that the reverberation does not become too strong and, at least, one still senses the rests.

Sonata No. 10 in G major, Op. 96

If we keep to the letter of text, there are some pedalling indications in this Sonata which are hard to realise.

First Movement
From **bar 247** (two different chords with one pedal):

204

I will try to describe how I imagine this section. Apparently Beethoven would like to have the chromatic development from C major (**bar 240**) to G major (**bar 260**) executed without apparent terraced dynamics. The dialogue between the bass (pianoforte) and the violin part is interwoven with the continuous eighth-note line in the piano. The pedal – held as long as possible – supports the floating and gliding of the voices by creating a spatial effect.

The execution of this passage (difficult on today's instruments) suceeds more easily if one starts the first notes of the left hand in **bar 247** *pp*. The pedal, as in all similar passages, should be quite light, and changed only where it is written, except tor **bar 254**, where the pedal should already be lifted before the third quarter-note, as in **bar 250** and according to the manuscript.

Another possibility in **bar 247** would be to change the pedal on the third quarter-note, and play all notes in the right hand *legatissimo* (quasi *ped.*).

Second and Fourth Movements

Here also are some surprising and thought-provoking *ped.* signs, such as in **bars 10–11**:

bars 47–49, **54**, **56–59**, **65–67**:

and similarly **bars 172—173** in the fourth movement:

The breathing rests and the effect of hovering in space resulting from the prolonging of the pedal can best be realized (as in previous examples) by a minimal raising of the pedal (not a pedal change). If one wants to be exact one should not apply the pedal in **bar 54** until the second note, as is quite clearly indicated in the manuscript.

The result of applying Beethoven's pedal signs to the whole work leads us into a world of sound which is far removed from the conventional. The peculiarities and roughness which startle us cannot all be explained by Beethoven's deafness or by the different character of sound of the instruments of that time. The pedal signs surprise us less if we bring them into relationship with the vehement outbursts and constant changes of his mighty mind. A genius like Beethoven makes his own laws, both formally and aesthetically. For us there remains the almost insoluble task of representing the creations of his overwhelming imagination with the precision that he demands.

The rewards are worth the effort.

Ensemble Playing:
On Partnership

We have made progress: we now speak of duos, of ensemble playing. But the time is not long past when it was considered the greatest compliment for the 'accompanist' of the virtuoso player, even in sonatas, to say that he was adaptable, that he was not too loud. The casually dropped remark of a concert-goer that the pianist might perhaps have been just a little too loud means he has failed to appreciate everything that the poor fellow had produced in the course of the evening in terms of imagination and power of performance.

It is true that the string player's apprehensions about the grand piano, especially of the open lid, are still widespread and sometimes loom so large that the reduction of the piano sound to a dynamic minimum becomes the most important issue in rehearsal, and one must put up with the monotony and paleness of expression which then arise. Adaptability and restraint in dynamics and expression here become the essential qualities in performance. But is this what the composer had in mind for his composition?

A modern concert grand with its customary brilliant tone is not, in fact, the ideal instrument for the duo sonatas of classical literature. The pianos of Beethoven's time had less volume of sound and were more transparent in the bass, although the leather hammers produced a harder tone. We must start with the consideration of how to make music on our contemporary instruments. The piano should not be too big, nor the voicing too brilliant. There can be no question that ensemble playing with string players demands much more mastery of touch differentiation on the modern grand piano than on the old instruments. The gradation of the dynamic between pp and mf must be shaded with real precision.

Restraint in the range f to ff must not be at the expense of expression.

But it is not enough to make one-sided concessions. The problem cannot be solved by closing the lid of the grand piano and by accommodation on one side only. One does not arrive at a genuine balance by eliminating some of the qualities of the piano. As long as the violinist plays dynamically as if he were in a string quartet, frustration will arise (the composer of duo sonatas certainly did not have a string quartet in his mind's ear). Just as the pianist must govern himself according to the possibilities in sound and dynamics of the stringed instrument, the violinist should take account of the nature of the piano.

The Sonatas we are dealing with here are duos, dialogues – call them what you will. The prerequisites for musically satisfactory ensemble playing are strong and secure partners, both of whom are in complete command of their own part as well as of the whole score. Both players must base themselves primarily on the score. It is the sound of the composition that is the goal, not the simple combination of two voices. It is indispensable that both partners are able and ready to listen as well as to lead, have the capacity for tonal and dynamic gradation in all the regions of expression, the art of phrasing, flexibility, and a sure feeling for tempo. The technical command of the instruments should be no less than a virtuoso's.

Even with such prerequisites the joy of ideal ensemble playing is never a free gift. Even when there is spontaneous agreement at a first attempt at music-making, one needs a lot of time to rehearse, time to try several possibilities, to form a phrase, build up a climax, co-ordinate sound and dynamics, until each player feels comfortable with the version arrived at. All this demands as much passionate involvement with the work in hand as patience with each other.

Appendix

PERFORMANCE PROBLEMS IN THE INTERPRETATION OF CLASSICAL AND ROMANTIC MUSIC

Paul Rolland

The Mannheim, Haydn and Mozart Era

Our insight into an historically correct performance style is much aided by the detailed and clear instructions offered in four books: Geminiani's *The Art of Playing on the Violin* (1751),[1] J.J. Quantz' *Versuch einer Anweisung die Flöte Traversiere zu Spielen* (1751),[2] C. P. E. Bach's *Versuch über die wahre Art das Clavier zu Spielen* (1753),[3] and Leopold Mozart's *Gründliche Violinschule* (1756). Of these books, the violin method of Mozart's father is of the deepest interest to the string player, but the other works are also of real value in re-establishing the musical thinking of the early Classical period. Interestingly enough, the four works were published within five years, and no other work of similar import was to follow for some time thereafter.

These treatises offer valuable information on musical style and performance in the 18th century. The last of the four books was published in the year of Mozart's birth; the information contained and principals established therein should hold true for some time thereafter, for musical tastes and performance habits change slowly and gradually. Hence it is safe to assume that the principles voiced in all four books remained valid until about the time of Beethoven's

[1] A facsimile edition (ed. David D. Boyden) was published by Oxford University Press, London, in 1969.

[2] Facsimile of 3rd edn. (Berlin, 1789), ed. Hans-Peter Schmitz, Documenta Musicologica, Vol. 2, Bärenreiter, Cassel, 1953.

[3] *Essay on the True Art of Playing Keyboard Instruments*, trans. and ed. William J. Mitchell, Cassell, London, 1949; reprinted by Eulenburg Books, London, 1974.

[4] Facsimile of 3rd edn. (1787), VEB Deutscher Verlag für Musik, Leipzig, 1968; *A Treatise on the Fundamental Principles of Violin Playing*, trans. Editha Knocker, Oxford University Press, London, 1948.

first period and were gradually forgotten and replaced by practices that in degrees began to approach and resemble the typical musical performance of today.

Tone Production
in the 17th and 18th centuries

The writings of Geminiani and Leopold Mozart make it quite obvious that our contemporary concept of an evenly sustained tone, with well-camouflaged changes of bow, was unknown. Instead, each stroke had its individual life, so to say, with generous use of swells, *crescendi* and *diminuendi*. Mozart's concept of the four bow divisions is notable in this connection.

First Division
'Begin the down or up stroke with a pleasant softness, increase the tone by means of an imperceptible increase of pressure; let the greatest volume of tone occur in the middle of the bow, after which, moderate it by degrees, by relaxing the pressure of bow until at the end of the bow the tone dies completely away.' The formula here is: weak–strong–weak.

Second Division
The formula here is: strong–decrease–weak.

Third Division
Weak–increase–strong.

Fourth Division
Weak–strong–weak–strong–weak.

Evenly Sustained Tone
'But besides this, a very useful *experiment* may be made. Namely, to endeavour to produce a perfectly even tone with a slow stroke. Draw the bow from one end to the other whilst sustaining throughout an even strength of tone. But hold the bow well back, for the longer and more even the stroke can be made, the more you will become master of your bow, which is highly necessary for the proper performance of a slow piece.'

Tone Beginning and Ending
'Every tone, even the strongest attack, has a gentle even if barely audible softness at the beginning of the stroke. This same softness must be heard also at the end of each stroke. Hence, one must know how to divide the bow into weakness and strength, and therefore

how by means of pressure and relaxation to produce the notes beautifully and touchingly.'

On Slurred Notes

'If in a composition 2, 3, 4 or more notes be slurred together . . . one recognizes that the composer wishes the notes not to be separated but played singingly in one slur. The first of such united notes must be somewhat more strongly stressed, but the remainder slurred onto it quite smoothly and more quietly.

'The first of 2, 3, 4 or even more notes, slurred together, must at all times be stressed more strongly, and sustained a little longer; but those following must diminish in tone and be slurred on somewhat later. . . . But this must be carried out with such good judgment that the bar length is not altered. The slight sustaining of the first note must not only be made agreeable to the ear by a nice apportioning of the slightly hurried notes slurred onto it, but must even be made truly pleasant to the listener.

'In the same way, when uneven notes occur which are slurred together, the longer notes must not be made too short, but rather sustained a little over long, and such passages shall be played singingly and with sound judgment.

'A short note followed by a long one must be frequently slurred to it, in which case the short note is always played quickly, not hurried, but so slurred onto the longer note that the whole weight falls on the latter.'

On Slurred Pairs

'The first of two notes coming together in one stroke is accented stronger and held slightly longer, while the second is slurred onto it quite quietly and rather late.'

On Ties

'. . . such notes must be attacked strongly (syncopations) and with a gradual dying away, be sustained without after pressure; just as the sound of a bell, when struck sharply, by degrees dies away.'

Alteration of Rhythm

C. P. E. Bach, Quantz and Leopold Mozart were in agreement that certain rhythmic patterns were not played as written. The most typical rhythmic alterations follow.

Leopold Mozart speaking of dotted notes: 'The dot must be joined on the note with a gradual fading away, and must never be distinguished by means of an accent.

'In quick pieces the bow is lifted at each dot. Therefore each note is separated from the other and performed in singing style.

'There are certain passages in slow pieces where the dot must be held rather longer . . . if the performance is not to sound too sleepy. For if the dot were held its usual length it would sound very languid and sleepy. In such case dotted notes must be held somewhat longer, but the time taken up by the extended value, must be, so to speak, stolen from the note standing after the dot. The dot should in fact be held at all times somewhat longer than its value. Not only is the performance thereby enlivened, but hurrying – that almost universal fault – is thereby checked. It would be a good thing if this long retention of the dot were insisted and set down as a rule. I, at least, have often done so, and I have made clear my opinion of the right manner of performance by setting down two dots followed by a shortened note.'

Quantz writes: 'I must . . . make a necessary remark concerning the length of time that each note must be held'. In other words, he felt it necessary to explain how the played values deviated from the written ones. Today the absolute value of notes is expressed in the notation, but early notation was a mere approximation of the musical idea. Then Quantz elaborates further how in slow tempo the 'good notes' (i.e., those requiring an accent) are played a little longer than the 'bad' offbeats, passing notes. He further gives examples of slurred pairs, where the first note should be held somewhat longer. In 'short-longs' he recommends that the short note be always shorter than its written value. This rule is modified by C. P. E. Bach and Daniel Gottlob Türk in his *Clavierschule* (1789),[5] saying that this is *not always* so, especially in slow movements. Emanuel Bach suggests that the sixteenths in the figure ♫ ♫ and similar 'sound insipid in an *adagio* if dots are not placed between them'.

The 'Lombard Snap'

Slurred pairs ♫ were often played ♫. , mostly in descending figures and in lively pieces. J. S. Bach has several 'errors' writing one or the other pattern within the same piece and in the same theme.

---

[5] *Clavierschule, oder Anweisung zum Clavierspielen für Lehrer and Lernende*, facsimile edn., ed. Erwin R. Jacobi, Documenta Musicologica, Series 1, Vol. 23, Bärenreiter, Cassel, 1962; *School of Clavier Playing*, trans. and ed. Raymond H. Haggh, University of Nebraska Press, Lincoln, Nebraska, 1982.

Accents

Leopold Mozart states that when half-notes are mixed with shorter values, it is customary to accent the former strongly, then relax the tone on the faster notes. The same goes for quarter-notes when played with eighths and sixteenths. 'In lively pieces the accent is mostly used on the highest note, in order to make the performance right merry.'

Rubato in the Classical Period

Contrary to widespread belief and practices, alteration of rhythm was not the only deviation from the written score. Both Carl Philip Emanuel Bach and Wolfgang Mozart speak of *rubato* in their writings, but only of the kind in which 'the left hand does not know what the right hand is doing' (on the keyboard). In this type of *rubato* the left hand plays in strict time but the right hand is permitted to wander within reason. They are opposed to changing the rhythm of the accompaniment. C. P. E. Bach: 'If the executant upon the clavier manages matters in such a way that one hand appears to play *against* time whilst the other strictly observes the beat, then the *right thing* has been done. In such a case the parts rarely move simultaneously but they fit together all the same'.

While rhythmic alteration went out of fashion in Beethoven's time, his music was not played as cut and dried as the proponents of the *Neue Sachlichkeit* (New Objectivity) of this century would have it. The German *Bauhaus*-type architecture (a style of smooth geometrical lines in architecture in reaction against the Victorian) parallels the seeking of long unbroken lines in musical construction and performance. But Czerny, a long-time student and associate of Beethoven, has this to say: 'Every composition must be played in the tempo prescribed by the composer and adhered to by the executant, notwithstanding, however, that in almost every line there are certain notes and passages where a little *ritardando* or *accelerando* is necessary, to beautify the reading and to augment the interest'. Czerny's rules on *ritardando* are remarkable:

1. At the return of the main subject.
2. When a phrase is to be separated from a melody.
3. On long notes strongly accented.
4. At a transition to a different time.
5. After a pause.
6. On the *diminuendo* of a quick, lively passage.
7. Where the ornamentation cannot be played *tempo giusto* (strictly).
8. In a well marked *crescendo* introducing or finishing a subject.

9. In passages where the composer and performer gives free play to his fancy.

10. When the composer marks his passage *espressivo* [!].

11. At the end of a shake or cadence.

The introduction of such frequent and unwritten *ritardandi* as suggested by Czerny is significant. The ideas of Beethoven's student and close associate are far removed from contemporary streamlined performance practices.

Tempo

Quantz sets objective standards by relating tempo and the human heartbeat, which pulses approximately 80 times per minute. This beat is then designated as quarter-note in *moderato*, as eighth in slow tempo, and as half-note or dotted half in fast movements. He speaks of a beat half again as fast as the heartbeat (i.e., 120 beats per minute) as typical in the most common type of *allegro*. Quantz' tempo is quite fast by today's standards of baroque works. Most likely the increased demands for tone and perfection of intonation slow down the contemporary player.

Dances show a tendency of getting slower with successive generations. Bach's minuet was fast, and Haydn's is rustic, lively and vigorous as a rule; but Mozart's minuet is courtly and slower. The slowed minuet was the likely cause of Beethoven's creation of a new, faster dance movement – the scherzo.

Vibrato

Leopold Mozart, Geminiani and other early writers acknowledge vibrato. According to Mozart, '. . . the finger of the left hand should make a small, *slow* movement which must not be sideways but forward and backward. That is, the finger must move toward the bridge and scroll: in soft tone slowly, but in loud tone rather faster'.

Geminiani has been criticized for his eccentric use of too frequent vibrato. Nevertheless, vibrato was not employed constantly as it is today. Paganini marked vibrato occasionally in his manuscripts. The Joachim Quartet was criticised for its 'constant use of vibrato' – which by today's standards must have been quite sporadic. Recordings of Joachim, Sarasate, Ysaÿe, Kubelík and even the young Szigeti show a different concept of vibrato, soon to be changed by the rising Kreisler.

Form

In the Classical period new forms of composition are created that dominate music to the present day. While a Baroque piece generally entertains a single idea or subject, the new sonata form brings a variety of ideas, moods within one movement. The various themes in this extended form should be of varied expression. In well written pieces the main theme and secondary theme are of contrasting character and mood. Above all, this variety of expression must be brought out in the new form with a consciousness of symmetry in form. The tempo must be such that it allows the various themes their proper expression. A composition is of good form where the best expression of its themes is possible in the same tempo. This unity of tempo, however, was not sought in the early Classical period: Leopold Mozart makes the (now) astonishing statement that when the theme recapitulates, or when repeating a section, one should play a little faster in order to keep the audience from falling asleep. This and other evidence make it clear that strictness of tempo throughout a movement was not originally demanded as it is today.

The variation of expression gives rise to the need for more tone colours and new sonorities unknown in the Baroque period, culminating in the writings of the impressionists.

Transition into the Romantic Period

Gradually the rules of Quantz and Mozart *père* go out of fashion. Türk in his 1789 piano method warns against the habit of changing the written value of notes. The changes in fashion gradually take hold in Beethoven's lifetime. His early works, those reflecting the Rococo spirit, should – perhaps – still have the earmarks of earlier practices; his later works, and those more Romantic in spirit, should not. The notation is becoming exact and binding.

Dynamics
Musical compositions of the Mannheim, Haydn and Mozart periods show a relatively light tonal texture. The violins of the period still had the original short necks, their tone was less loud and not so brilliant. The piano was also a smaller, more delicate instrument. The player was sensitive to the acoustic properties of the room, and played softer in smaller rooms, projected his tone more in larger rooms. It is not in style to play Mozart with vigorous Brahmsian dynamics. The contrasts between soft and loud passages should not be extreme, but the use of obvious *crescendo* and *decrescendo* is justified.

Beethoven widens the dynamic range; his scores from his middle period on are explicit in demanding dynamics that range from *pp* to *ff*. His heavier texture demands more tone, his piano parts and orchestrations are heavier.

The Romantic traits of adventure and surprise are emphasized by sudden changes of dynamics: *crescendo* leading to sudden (*subito*) *piano* or *pianissimo*. Increased tonal demands lead to the general acceptance of the new inward curved bow, which is more suitable for a more sustained type of tone production. The Romantic themes increase in length, and require a more linear, sustained tone. The offbeats, passing notes – formerly played with courtly elegance and brevity – become sustained, even prolonged and intensive. In the compositions of Brahms and the later Romantics the offbeats and passing notes should be played expressively, without lightening the tone. The increased harmonic richness and generally heavier texture results in a search for increased sonorities. The violin necks are lengthened, pitch is rising and Wilhelmj's tone becomes the ideal with its tremendous intensity. The rich harmonic texture cuts off the softest dynamics formerly employed in solo performance.

Composers become aware of the problems of balance in ensemble and orchestra writing and abandon the principle of block-dynamics in their scoring; instead they would designate various dynamics to individual parts played concurrently. The vibrato is used as an ornamental asset to enhance the expression *at proper places*. On the other hand, the *portamento* is used in abundance and in conformity with the (then) correct rules of shifting always sliding on the 'old finger'.

The increased tonal demands bring the *détaché*, *martelé* types of bowing into the foreground at the expense of the light, lifted *spiccato* types. Ignaz Moscheles, a prominent composer and critic of the Schumann era, criticises a violinist after his concert: his playing is old-fashioned, he bounces and lifts the bow so much.

Musical expression now gains in passion and in pathos but loses much of its natural charm and humour. The typical Romantic performer is passionate, bold and serious as well as sentimental, but he has lost much of his humour.

Tempo

Mälzel's invention of the metronome was initially hailed by Beethoven enthusiastically. His own metronome markings of some of his compositions are fast by today's standards. Later he grew distrustful of the machine due to an incident when he lost a copy of music with his metronome markings: when the lost copy was found, his earlier and later metronome markings were completely different. From then on he distrusted the metronome and denied the existence of a 'correct' tempo; instead, the tempo should suit the occasion and the individual performer.

Mendelssohn is described by his contemporaries as one who likes fluent tempi, and speed. Brahms' tempi, by comparison, must have been quite slow. Teachers of this writer, and artists like Enescu and Casals, who all heard Brahms' playing, insisted upon the very moderate speed of his *allegro* movements.

Slow movements are also getting slower. While Leopold Mozart designates about the same speed to an *andante* and *allegretto*, the Romantic *andante* and *adagio* are so slow that the earlier designations of *adagio molto*, *largo*, *lento* and *grave* all but disappear during the Romantic period.

Romantic Rubato
Beethoven's contemporaries state that in his later years he played 'with few exceptions free of all restraint in tempo: a *tempo rubato* in the most exact meaning of the term'. But this manner of playing did not appear until his last period.

Thus a more lavish and flexible *rubato* appears, one that breaks down the strict rule of beats and bar-lines, one, in which the left hand *knows* what the right hand is doing, and follows it, unlike the ways of Mozart and C. P. E. Bach. Thus the emotional lift of a *crescendo* is augmented by a concurrent *accelerando*, and to make a *diminuendo* more lethargic, a *ritenuto* is also employed. Such agogic freedom is the chief characteristic of the Romantic period, and without it the works of Schumann, Chopin and Liszt become meaningless. It seems, though, that the music of composers of chamber and orchestral music (Schubert, Mendelssohn, Brahms) is not nearly as free as that of their piano composer colleagues, possibly due to the limitations of ensemble problems. Nevertheless, it must be obvious that a historically correct Romantic performance is much more flexible than the objective style now often heard, which is a reaction to the exaggerated tendencies of the late Romantic performers.

Coda

Contemporary sources are helpful in developing a reasonably true style in the performance of the early masters. An obvious and more immediate helping device can be found in the performer's own imagination. If he visualizes the people – their manners, appearance, living conditions, attitudes – in the period in which the composer lived, his performance is likely to become more authentic.

Such visual images may come from the works of arts, from books, the theatre, and even from movies. Such images will suggest that the masters of the Baroque and early Classical period were highly cultured craftsmen, and solid citizens as a rule, in the employment of the aristocracy. Their social standing was low, although in some cases they were well cared for by their benefactors. Their manners were polite and refined, their behaviour humble, and perhaps servile. It was their task to create beautiful music for the enjoyment of'their benefactors, and to perform the same for entertainment, and not for the glorification of their own excellence and skill. As such, their music was highly functional, written for the present, and for the occasion. Their performing attitude perhaps could be described best by the words of Dmitry Merejkowsky:[6] the artist's soul is like a mirror that reflects the true beauties of the world, yet remaining pure and unaffected.

The later Classical masters were less well cared for. Long-time court appointments were unusual, and the musicians had to make ends meet as well as they could, by occasional commissions and teaching the families of noblemen. They also became more independent, and soon the Romantic performer appears, independent, erratic and arrogant. He appeals not only to the aristocracy but to the rising citizenry whose favours he seeks, tastes he serves. His performance is a mixture of beauty and wizardry; he must be sensational, unusual and astonishing to ensure his success. He is a man of the world, a lady-killer, he lives high and hard, and as a rule, not very long.

Romanticism, the inborn trait of the southern peoples – who speak the romance languages – reaches its height in music in the Germanic countries. It is the artist's yearning for the life of the Latin, for the country of warmth, where life is beautiful and 'where the orange and lemon grow'. The wishful thinking of the systematic, organized German-educated man for an adventurous, interesting life, in which individual emotions are given free expression was the motivation that moved the great Romantic composers. In their music, the individualistic, romantic element should be brought out, without indulging in excessive sentimentality, and within the limits of good taste.

---

[6] *The Romance of Leonardo da Vinci*, trans. Bernard Guilbert Guerney, Cassell, London, 1931.

214

BIBLIOGRAPHY

Extensive and useful bibliographical information can be found in the book *Beethoven Abstracts* prepared by Donald W. MacArdle just before his death in 1964 and published by Information Coordinators, Detroit, 1973, and in William Drabkin's bibliography in *The New Grove Dictionary of Music and Musicians*, Vol. 2, Macmillan, London, 1980, pp. 410–414. Other valuable titles and essays are listed below.

EMILY ANDERSON (transl. and ed.), *The Letters of Beethoven*, 3 vols., Macmillan, London/St Martin's Press, New York, 1961.

BERNHARD BARTELS, *Beethoven*, Meister der Musik No. 1, Franz Borgmeyer Verlag, Hildesheim, 1927.

BÉLA BARTÓK, Violin Concerto No. 2, Boosey & Hawkes, London/New York, 1941/1946.

LUDWIG VAN BEETHOVEN, Conversation Books (*Konversationshefte*) Vols. 1–8, ed. Karl-Heinz Köhler and Gritta Herre, VEB Deutscher Verlag für Musik, Leipzig, 1972–81.

PAUL BEKKER, *Beethoven*, J.M. Dent, London, 1927.

HECTOR BERLIOZ, *Voyage Musical en Allemagne et Italie*, Labitte, Paris, 1844; republished by Gregg International Publisher, Farnborough, Hampshire, 1970.

ROBERT BORY, *Ludwig van Beethoven: His Life and Work in Pictures*, Thames & Hudson, London, 1966.

DAVID D. BOYDEN, *The History of Violin Playing from its Origins to 1761*, Oxford University Press, London, 1965.

SIEGHARD BRANDENBURG, 'Bemerkungen zu Beethovens Op. 96', *Beethoven Jahrbuch 1977*, Beethoven-Haus, Bonn.

FREDERICK DORIAN, *The History of Music in Performance*, Norton, New York, 1942.

EDWIN FISCHER, *Beethoven's Pianoforte Sonatas*, Faber, London, 1959.

CARL FLESCH, *The Art of Violin Playing*, 2 vols., Fischer, New York, 1924–39.

NIGEL FORTUNE, 'The Chamber Music with Piano', in (ed.) Denis Arnold and Nigel Fortune, *The Beethoven Companion*, Faber, London, 1971.

GEORG KINSKY and HANS HALM (eds.), *Das Werk Beethovens*, Henle, Munich, 1955.

LUIGI MAGNANI, *I Quaderni di Conversazione di Beethoven*, Ricciardi, Milan, 1962.

PAUL NATORP, *Beethoven und Wir*, N.G. Elwertsche Verlagsbuchhandlung (G. Braun), Marburg an der Lahn, 1921.

RICHARD PETZOLD, *Ludwig van Beethoven*, VEB Deutscher Verlag für Musik, Leipzig, 1976.

RAINER RIEHN, 'Beethoven: Das Problem der Interpretation', *Musik-Konzepte*, 8, April, 1979.

HUGO RIEMANN, *Music Lexicon*, Augener, London, 1902–8 (12th German edn., Schott, Mainz, 1959–67); two-volume edn., Brockhaus, Wiesbaden/Schott, Mainz, 1979.

WALTER RIEZLER, *Beethoven*, Forrester, London, 1938.

ROMAIN ROLLAND, *Beethoven the Creator*, Gollancz, London, 1929.

ANTON FELIX SCHINDLER, *Beethoven as I Knew Him*, ed. Donald W. MacArdle, Faber, London/ University of North Carolina Press, Chapel Hill, North Carolina, 1966.

LEOPOLD SCHMIDT, *Beethoven: Werke und Leben*, Volksverband der Bücherfreunde, Wegweiser Verlag, Berlin, 1924.

BORIS SCHWARZ, 'Beethoven and the French Violin School', *The Musical Quarterly*, Vol. XLIV, No. 4, October 1958.

ROBIN STOWELL, *Violin Technique and Performance Practice in the Late Eighteenth and Early Nineteenth Centuries*, Cambridge University Press, Cambridge, 1985.

J.W.N. SULLIVAN, *Beethoven*, Life and Letters Series No. 15, Jonathan Cape, London, 1930.

JOSEPH SZIGETI, *The Ten Beethoven Sonatas for Piano and Violin*, ed. Paul Rolland, American String Teachers' Association, Urbana (Illinois), 1965.

ALEXANDER WHEELOCK THAYER, *Life of Beethoven*, ed. Elliot Forbes, Princeton University Press, 1964 (ed. Hermann Deiters, Breitkopf & Härtel, Leipzig, 1901).

W.A. THOMAS-SAN-GALLI, *Ludwig van Beethoven*, R. Piper Verlag, Munich, 1913.

DONALD FRANCIS TOVEY, *Beethoven*, Oxford University Press, London, 1944.

ALAN TYSON, *The Authentic English Editions of Beethoven*, Faber, London, 1963.

RICHARD WAGNER, *Beethoven*, Reeves, London, 1880.

JUSTUS HERMANN WETZEL, *Beethovens Violinsonaten*, Max Hesses Verlag, Berlin, 1924.

INDEX

Page numbers in bold type indicate detailed discussion of a work or illustration of an individual.

THE MUSIC OF FRANZ SCHMIDT
Volume One: The Orchestral Music
HAROLD TRUSCOTT
With 'Personal Recollections' by
Hans Keller
And the 'Autobiographical Sketch' of
Franz Schmidt

Franz Schmidt is one of the great composers. His music covers symphonies, quartets, opera and oratorio, music for piano and organ, and his work in all of these fields reveals a master of large-scale symphonic form and one of the most substantial lyric geniuses of all time. Born in Hungary in 1874, Schmidt spent most of his life in Austria and is occasionally referred to as 'the Austrian Elgar', but despite his undeniable stature, he has not yet received the attention he deserves. Now this first of a three-volume series from Toccata Press brings to Schmidt's music the scholarship it so richly merits: Harold Truscott, an authority on Schmidt and many other composers, and himself an important composer, examines his orchestral music – the four powerful Symphonies, the *Variations on a Hussar Song* and the *Chaconne* – taking the reader and listener through each of these great masterpieces.

This first volume is introduced by the 'Personal Recollections' of Hans Keller, who knew Schmidt well in pre-World-War-II Vienna. The book also carries the first-ever translation into English of Schmidt's *Autobiographical Sketch*, where the composer tells of his early childhood in Hungary, his teenage years near Vienna, his life as a cellist in the Vienna Philharmonic Orchestra and his conflict with Gustav Mahler.

The Music of Franz Schmidt: Volume One is an early step in the rediscovery of one of the towering figures of our age. It is not so long since Bruckner and Mahler were rescued from the neglect they never deserved. Now it is Schmidt's turn.

'Schmidt's music is superbly and unarguably well made, in unhurried Brucknerian spans, and richly melodic . . . . it is . . . described in loving detail which will whet musical appetites for the unrecorded symphonies. Toccata Press does great service to the cause – and, one hopes, the real revival of interest . . .'
David Murray, *Financial Times*

192pp; index
£9.95 (hardcover)

BOULT ON MUSIC
Words from a Lifetime's Communication
SIR ADRIAN BOULT
With a Foreword by
Bernard Shore
and an Introduction by
Vernon Handley

One of this century's best-loved conductors, Sir Adrian Boult
often wrote and broadcast on music during the course of his
long life. His style of expression, whether writing, speaking or
conducting, was always concerned with directness of
communication. *Boult on Music* assembles the most important of
Sir Adrian's broadcast essays and talks, exploring many
aspects of his art. He discusses composers he knew and worked
with, like Elgar and Vaughan Williams, as well as such figures
as Schubert and Bach. He examines the craft of his conductor
colleagues, like Toscanini, Wood, Nikisch and Beecham, and of
fellow musicians like Menuhin and Casals. He also turns his
attention to the problems and practicalities of the conductor's
task.

Bernard Shore, for many years Sir Adrian's Principal Viola
in the BBC Symphony Orchestra and a distinguished writer on
music, has contributed a Foreword on 'The Art of Sir Adrian';
and Vernon Handley, whom many regard as Sir Adrian's
successor as the most important conductor of British music,
introduces *Boult on Music*, assembled as a tribute to this great
and modest man.

'There is no doubt that this was a collection worth making . . . .
here are wisdom and kindness – two qualities which all who
knew Sir Adrian will instantly recognise'
Jerrold Northrop Moore, *Times Literary Supplement*

'Never dull, often illuminating' *Southern Evening Echo*

'wisdoms worth long pondering'
Michael Oliver, *The Gramophone*

Musicians on Music No. 1
196pp; index
£9.95 (hardcover)
£4.95 (softcover)

THE PROMS AND NATURAL JUSTICE
A Plan for Renewal
ROBERT SIMPSON
With a Foreword by
Sir Adrian Boult

In this important and provocative book Robert Simpson, for nearly thirty years a BBC Music Producer, scrutinises the methods by which the Proms are planned.

At present, the BBC allows the Controller, Music the absolute right to decide Prom programmes until death or retirement. Basing his reasoning on long experience inside the BBC, Dr Simpson argues that whoever the Controller might be, the effects of his individuality are bound to colour the programmes over time. The only logical way to give the Proms the flair that a single imagination can provide — without the otherwise inevitable long-term imbalances affecting both composers and performers — is to appoint a separate planner of the Proms with a limited tenure of four or five years.

Dr Simpson further examines the artistic gains and financial savings to be made from more extensive use of the BBC's own orchestras. Not only would this produce a saving of a staggering 62% on present costs — it would give the planner almost total control over the repertoire. This would enable the Proms to become more adventurous than ever before — a true realisation of Sir Henry Wood's original vision.

'constructive and principled criticism from one of our finest musicians'   Leader, *Daily Telegraph*

'convincing and fierce'   *The Guardian*

'all who are interested in this great annual festival and its future should read this book'   Sir Adrian Boult

vi+66pp; index
£1.95

STRAVINSKY SEEN AND HEARD
Hans Keller and Milein Cosman

In *Stravinsky Seen and Heard* Hans Keller and Milein Cosman concentrate on two different aspects of this multi-faceted composer.

Hans Keller analyses not only Stravinsky's conversion to serial technique but also those elements in his creative character, never yet touched upon, which made this dramatic change of mind possible.

Milein Cosman, who has long been known for her portrayal of musicians in action, contributes an extended series of over 60 drawings of Stravinsky at rehearsal, full of life and movement. Hans Keller's discoveries are thus complemented, throwing new light on one of the longest-established geniuses of our age, who yet remains a subject of controversy.

Stravinsky Seen and Heard also contains a full analysis of Stravinsky's serial technique, as used in his Dylan Thomas setting, 'Do not go gentle'.

'this marvellous . . . stimulating, valuable and utterly unique book . . . which anyone who professes to care about the state of twentieth century art should possess'

Music and Musicians

'stimulating'   *Times Literary Supplement*

'It's a brilliant and absorbing essay and the pictures are marvellous — got the old reptile superbly!'

Robert Simpson

128pp; index
£3.95 (softcover)